THE NEW AMERICAN POETS

THE

Edited by Michael Collier

NEW

AMERICAN

POETS

A Bread Loaf Anthology

Bread Loaf Writers' Conference and Middlebury College Press

Published by University Press of New England

Hanover and London

Middlebury College Press
Published by University Press of New England, Hanover, NH 03755
© 2000 by Bread Loaf Writers' Conference/Middlebury College
Printed in the United States of America
5 4 3 2

About the Editor

MICHAEL COLLIER is the director of the Bread Loaf Writers' Conference. His most recent book of poems is *The Ledge* (Houghton Mifflin, 2000). He teaches at the University of Maryland.

Library of Congress Cataloging-in-Publication Data

The new American poets: A Bread Loaf anthology / edited by Michael Collier.
     p.   cm.
    "Bread Loaf Writer's Conference and Middlebury College Press."
    ISBN 0 – 87451 – 963 – 2 (alk. paper) — ISBN 0 – 87451 – 964 – 0 (pbk. : alk. paper)
    1. American poetry — 20th century.   I. Collier, Michael, 1953 –   . II. Bread Loaf
Writers' Conference of Middlebury College.
PS615.N383   2000
811'.5408 — dc21   99 – 56171

Grateful acknowledgment is made for permission to reprint the following poems:

Elizabeth Alexander, "Compass" and "Washington Etude," from *Body of Life*, 1996, Tia Chucha Press, A Project of the Guild Complex.
Molly Bendall, "A Painter of Destinies," is taken from the award-winning volume *After Estrangement* by Molly Bendall (Salt Lake City, Utah: Gibbs-Smith Publisher, 1992). Used with permission. "Fete on the Lake" and "The Book of Sharp Silhouettes," from *Dark Summer*, 1999, Miami University Press. Used with permission.
David Biespiel, "Tower" copyright © 1996 by David Biespiel. Reprinted from *Shattering Air* with the permission of BOA Editions, Ltd.
Richard Blanco, "Shaving," "Letter to El Flaco on His Birthday," "The Silver Sands," "Last Night in Havana," and "Tia Olivia Serves Wallace Stevens a Cuban Egg" are from CITY OF A HUNDRED FIRES, by Richard Blanco, © 1998. Reprinted by permission of the University of Pittsburgh Press.
Nick Carbó, "I Found Orpheus Levitating," from *El Grupo McDonald's*, 1995, Tia Chucha Press.
Leslie Dauer, "Falling" and "The Woman in the Film," from *Fragile City*, 1996, Bluestem Press, Emporia State University.
Debra Kang Dean, "Stitches," "Immigrants," "Back to Back," "Taproot," copyright © 1998, by Debra Kang Dean. Reprinted from *News of Home* with the permission of BOA Editions, Ltd.
Jill Alexander Essbaum, "In the Beginning," "Post-Communion Striptease," "When the Kingdom Comes," and "Paradise," from *Heaven*, University Press of New England, forthcoming.

continued on page 281

For Robert and David

Contents

Acknowledgments

I owe debts to a number of people and institutions who have encouraged and supported this project. Mary Jo Bang, Edward Hirsch, Garrett Hongo, James Longenbach, Jacqueline Osherow, Stanley Plumly, David St. John, Tom Sleigh, Michael Theune, and Ellen Bryant Voigt made generous suggestions. The staff at the University Press of New England has provided its welcomed expertise. Middlebury College provided its singular belief in the importance of literary endeavors. I am particularly grateful to Kellie Tabor for her capable and friendly assistance. Lastly, my thanks to Katherine, Robert, and David for their patience and love.

M.C.

Preface

Pluralism and eclecticism mark the poetry in this anthology of new American poets and distinguish it from the poetry of the seventies, eighties, and early nineties, which often found itself at odds with the experiments of Language-based poets, the New Formalist revivications, or the poetry of identity and politics. The poets collected in these pages are characterized by a sympathy for and attraction to various aesthetics. This sympathy is an achievement that is peculiarly American, an achievement that recognizes that, while the country may contain many different, even antagonistic attitudes concerning poetry, their destination is unity or, if not quite unity, then conversation and dialog. With very few exceptions, the fifty-six poets included here are forty years of age and under or they have published a first book of poems within the last five years. While a number of the poets in the volume have attended the Bread Loaf Writers' Conference in the past, most have not. They are curious about the multi-voiced idiom of contemporary American poetry, and they follow their curiosity with the freedom and lack of self-consciousness we expect of a new generation. But "generation" is a curious word to use to describe these poets who range in age from mid-twenties to early fifties. This generation, itself made up of generations, is one of the most hopeful and interesting developments to have taken place in American poetry since the 1970s. It challenges the notion that freshness, innovation, and risk are qualities available primarily to the young or that the vocation of a poet declares itself early in one's life and is ever afterward unavoidable. The poets collected here not only comprise a unique and surprising anthology of new American poets, but they express the hope and future of the art.

In 1900 when Edmund Clarence Stedman wrote the "Prelude to *An American Anthology*" for his survey of American poetry from 1787 to 1899, he proclaimed, in a trimmed-around-the-ears version of Whitman, to have seen "the constelled matin choir" of American poetry singing "together in the dawn." He envisaged a soul train of poets that wound its way from old to young, singing "for joy / Of mount and wood and cataract, and stretch / Of keen-aired vasty reaches happy-homed." I bring Stedman up to caution myself—especially since *The New American Poets* appears not only at the turn of a century but at the change of a millennium—against making claims of "keen-aired vasty reaches" for its poets. The optimism and enthusiasm of Stedman's "Prelude" is a cant we expect now mainly from politicians. Nevertheless, readers of American poetry at the turn of this century can revel in an optimism born of the healthy and proliferating state of the art. This art is the fruition of the many experiments and developments that began to appear in American poetry and culture in the 1950s. It is also an art that gainsays the once popular complaint that poetry has no relevant relationship to the world around it and that poets were somehow to blame for this state. The very multiplicity of the work collected here speaks to the wide and various constituencies of imagination alive in American culture. Beyond what I've ventured above about the future of contemporary American poetry, it is difficult to make predictions, though millennial fever demands a phrase or two of prognostication. The lively energy of the poets in *this* "American Anthology" attests to the vitality of the poetic art, and in this respect I hear in them what Stedman heard in his constellated choir: the "impassioned song" of the future.

The anthology also marks the seventy-fifth anniversary of the Bread Loaf Writers' Conference. The Conference's most important mission is to support new and emerging writers. "New" poets who once attended Bread Loaf include Theodore Roethke, John Ciardi, May Swenson, Robert Francis, Anne Sexton, X. J. Kennedy, Miller Williams, Ellen Bryant Voigt, Edward Hirsch, Rita Dove, Carolyn Forché, David St. John, Alice Fulton, Garrett Hongo, Gjertrude Schnackenberg, Cornelius Eady, Tom Sleigh, and many more. Each year, through its fellowship and scholarship program and the Katharine Bakeless Nason Literary Publication Prize, Bread Loaf hosts many of the best new and emerging American poets. One of the privileges of directing the Conference is the opportunity I have each year of meeting these poets and seeing the ways in which they are reshaping American poetry for the twenty-first century. The publication of *The New American Poets* during the seventy-fifth anniversary of the Conference underscores the commitment I have as Conference Director to the continuing role Bread Loaf will play in the next century to support the literary arts.

M.C.

THE NEW AMERICAN POETS

ELIZABETH ALEXANDER

ELIZABETH ALEXANDER is the author of two volumes of poems, *The Venus Hottentot* (University Press of Virginia, 1990) and *Body of Life* (Tia Chucha Press, 1996). She lives in New Haven, Connecticut.

Compass

I.

I swing
the thin tin
arm to mark
an arc
from pole
to pole: my
mother's compass
spans the world.
It marks
the globe from east
to west on this
white paper as
I twirl
the compass,
hear the hush
of graphite:
a horizon.

II.

It feels freest
at its widest set,
held just by a pin-
prick on the page,
moored and precarious,
like Mathew Henson's flag.

III.

Even the dogs died.
His Eskimo grandchildren cried

when, years later, the black man
they prayed was a Henson

came looking to figure
what makes a man hazard

ten lifetimes of snow. Hayden
imagined your arguments, hunger,

delirium. The fur of your hood
frames your brown face like petals or rays.

To stand where the top of the world curves.
To look all around in that silence.

To breathe in cold air that has never
been squandered, breathe out again.

To breathe in cold air, to breathe
in . . . out . . .

breathe in

Feminist Poem Number One

Yes I have dreams where I am rescued by men:
my father, brother, husband, no one else.
Last night I dreamed my brother and husband
morphed into each other and rescued me
from a rat-infested apartment. "Run!"
he said, feral scampering at our heels.
And then we went to lunch at the Four Seasons.

What does it mean to be a princess?
"I am what is known as an American Negro,"
my grandmother would say, when "international friends"
would ask her what she was. She'd roller-skate
to Embassy Row and sit on the steps of the embassies
to be certain the rest of the world was there.

What does it mean to be a princess?
My husband drives me at six a.m.
to the airport an hour away, drives home,
drives back when I have forgotten my passport.
What does it mean to be a prince? I cook
savory, fragrant meals for my husband
and serve him, if he likes, in front of the TV.
He cooks for me, too. I have a husband.

In the dream we run into Aunt Lucy,
who is waiting for a plane from "Abyssinia"
to bring her lover home. I am the one
married to an Abyssinian, who is already here. I am the one
with the grandmother who wanted to know the world.
I am what is known as an American Negro princess,
married to an African prince,
living in a rat-free apartment in New Haven,
all of it, all of it, under one roof.

Overture: Watermelon City

Philadelphia is burning and water-
melon is all that can cool it,
so there they are, spiked
atop a row of metal poles,
rolling on and off pickup trucks,
the fruit that grows longest,
the fruit with a curly tail, the cool fruit,
larger than a large baby, wide
as the widest green behind, wide
vermillion smile at the sizzling metropole.
Did I see this yesterday? Did I dream
this last night? The city is burning,
is burning for real.

When I first moved here I lived two streets over
from Osage, where it happened, twelve streets down.
I asked my neighbors, who described
the smell of smoke and flesh,
the city on fire for real.
How far could you see the flames?
How long could you smell the smoke?
Osage is narrow, narrow
like a movie set: urban eastern seaboard,
the tidy of people who work hard for very little.

Life lived on the porch,
the amphitheater street.
I live here, 4937 Hazel Avenue, West Philly.
Hello Adam and Ukee,
the boys on that block
who guarded my car, and me.
They called him Ukee because
as a baby he looked
like a eucalyptus leaf.
Hello holy rollers
who plug in their amps,
blow out the power in the building,
preach to the street from the stoop.

Hello, crack-head next-door neighbor
who raps on my door after midnight
needing money for baby formula,
she says, and the woman
who runs in the street
with her titties out, wailing.
Hello street. Hello ladies
who sweep their front porches each morning.
In downtown Philadelphia
there are many lovely restaurants,
reasonably-priced.
Chocolate, lemon ice,
and hand-filled cannolis
in South Philly.
Around the corner
at the New Africa Lounge
in West Philadelphia
we sweat buckets
to hi-life and zouk,
we burn.

Washington Etude

After rain, mushrooms
appear in the park
but you can not eat them.

1967,
the year of the locust.
They come to Northwest

Washington by millions
and for days I crunch
shed husks beneath my feet

as they rattle and hiss
their rage from the trees.
Baby teeth bite baby

onion grass and honey-
suckle nipples, tiny
tongue balancing

the clear, sweet drops.
I am a humming-
bird, a cat who laps

cream from a bowl.
Dandelions
are yellow one day,

white the next. A mud-
puddle surrounded
by brambles and black-

berries is where God lives.
Buttercups under
my chin tell me all

I need to know. Nothing
blue occurs naturally
in Washington, someone

says, and I believe it.
I'm put to bed
when it's still light

and hear other children
playing out my window,
watch daylight bow,

regard the flare
of blooming stars,
the cicada's maraca.

CRAIG ARNOLD

Sean Graff

CRAIG ARNOLD's book *Shells* was the 1998 selection for the Yale Series of Younger Poets. His poems have appeared in *The Best American Poetry 1998* (Scribner, 1998), *Poetry, The Yale Review, The Paris Review*, and *The New Republic*. He has been an Amy Lowell Poetry Traveling Scholar and recently received an NEA fellowship.

XX

Coming to bed I come upon them lying
still half-dressed, lips pressed, exchanging what seems an
hour's breath, tips of their middle fingers
      hooked in each other,

thrashing fish on a line, a lush purple
passage, legs slick with each other's liquid
laid across each other holding as much a-
      part as together—

Polishing the mirror, the Chinese call it.
Who can stand to stare at a pair of mirrors
long? They never saw me turning to leave them
      leisure to finish,

didn't notice the trespass. Is this the reason
men who caught the virgin huntress Diana
waist-deep in water, sporting with raw-boned
      maidens, were hunted,

turned to deer that their own dogs would drive them,
stuck with indignant arrows? Not for envy.
Not for hairy animal nature breaking
        in on the naked.

Beaten, the stag will wander away to nurse his
antler-gashes, whatever pain he suffers
not from his own extraneousness, the bitter
        thought that a rival

has what he may only imagine. Sappho,
you might agree how much like love is feeling
extra, this falling into what you'd call the
        usual symptoms:

uncontrollable shaking, chill like a fever's
fire creeping my skin, my breath sucked coming
thickly as theirs did—now I can't distinguish
        one from the other.

Could I ever, seventeen and a virgin,
girl flashing her tits at me at a party,
first and last I grasp at excitement only
        mixed with exclusion?

The Disembodied Voices of Women

trail you down the hall—issue
suddenly out of doors left open
fingerprints—personal
enough to serve in court as evidence

At the party the woman is introduced
as no really a professional screamer
She works in slasher films—voices-over
the bloodcurdling shrieks of women
being killed or surpassed or otherwise ill-used
apparently a talent not everyone possesses
in real life as in dreams

You tell her of your friend in Madrid to study
Her father worked in adult films
as of course he would being adult
and famous for his nine-inch member
scored her a job in post-production dubbing
flattening Spanish into Middle West
all illegal of course—he had connections

Soon the inevitable came to pass
as of course it must being inevitable
She found herself faking moans
to match the open / close mouth of the blonde
Daddy was doing on the screen
It was kind of weird at first she said

The woman is looking for her date
another drink the bathroom the ashtray
Say something funny quick

You wonder what they say in Spain at the moment of crisis
Is the language of orgasm international like Esperanto?
You never had occasion to find out
although you found Castilian thrilling
tongue threading the needle of the teeth

and babies know mother because they hear voices
before they grow ears there are vibrations
plucking chords on the spine
Even a voice without a source is comfort
through the womb—in the next room—over the phone
as being yes as being less than silence

My Love Is Sick

My love is sick—she has begun to turn
inward upon herself—body peeled back
a rubber glove off of a stranger hand
seen things growing so many sharp edges

My love is sick—she bleeds
with strange irregular terror hard contained
breathes bubbles into her own blood
The bottle mouth is chipped—where is the missing glass?

My love is sick and who can help? It is not I
that put this into her—I tell myself
it is not I—it does not help
either of us, the telling

My love is sick and I would hold her
about the collarbones—hold her down
if she would let me—but between our skins
a storm roars in a film of air

My love is sick and I am afraid—afraid
her fear is stronger than my fear for her
and so we are made separate by fear
and so we are afraid and not together

The Party She Outdid Herself

In the blue velvet gown nobody else could wear
she coaxes the boys back to her bedroom

to squeeze their bodies into her old prom dresses.
Pink taffeta, pearl-seeded ivory sheath,

starless black velour collared with gold thread
—she fits straps to unfinished shoulders

pulls out pads, does zips, lays her lipstick puckers
to mark her territory, cheek, neck, arm.

Tequila, salt & lime appointed neatly in hands
too big, made elegant by association,

her arm around each waist, her nip on each earlobe,
our hostess, genial octopus, torments us:

I love you in a dress. I love you even more
out of it. You're so much fun to flirt with.

Are you uncomfortable? Are you embarrassed?
Is that a blush I see? We blush on cue,

smile our edgy smiles, our wooly legs exposed,
between them blown the unfamiliar air.

She folds us together like a cake, our atoms bound
by the force of what she has on each of us

the grace with which she holds her peace, at least in public:
He'd never guess who's been bowing down

to kiss his girl's trim lips, how grim she laughs at him.
He can't keep it hard for anyone.

He can't imagine how ridiculous he looks
a spinster aunt in pearls & owl-rim glasses

missing stiff lace on the throat to complete the picture
—a clan of cannibals, elbowing for place,

an audience with the queen, quick to draw straws
from the fistful she holds to see who's dinner.

Darling, forgive me if I make a spectacle.
I can't speak for all of your geisha boys,

motherless dressup dolls with smoothed-over crotches,
your tomcats fat & neutered as we deserve.

But tell me—when our welcome wears out at last
as it must no matter how warm it seems,

when at last your china-blue eyes chill to brittle,
begin to give away too much, when at last

you gather the folds of yourself back to yourself
to a privacy unfailingly just fine

& the boys you know better than they know themselves
take the cue, shed your dresses & shoo,

will there be anyone you let stick around
to hold your hair up if you get sick,

to make you drink at least three glasses of water,
to turn back one corner of the quilt,

to go about the room & pinch the sputtering candles,
pick up the cups, the bottles, the crushed limes,

the shucked dresses, straighten & smooth & lay them spread
neatly at the foot of your double bed

to hang up as you please tomorrow morning or afternoon,
whenever you feel composed enough to roll out

wipe the blear from your eyes & take us on again?
Dress us up, gather us to your breast,

whisper come-ons without force or consequence
—still I'm sad when I see you share your bed

with all those dresses—pleats, tucks, folds, & gathers,
intimations of secrecy & texture,

a seam stretched, the hem of sleeve & neck still damp
from a body you've made up, costumed, posed,

trifled with & dismissed. How much less mess.
How easier to ruffle. How oh fabulous.

MARY JO BANG

Yuri Marder

MARY JO BANG's book *Apology for Want* (University Press of New England/Middlebury College, 1997) was awarded the 1996 Bakeless Prize and the 1998 Great Lakes Colleges Association New Writers Award. She has been the recipient of a "Discovery"/*The Nation* Award and a Hodder Fellowship from Princeton University. She has taught at Yale University, the New School, and the University of Montana and, since 1995, has been poetry coeditor at *Boston Review*. Her work has appeared in *The New Republic, The New Yorker, The Paris Review, New American Writing, Denver Quarterly, Volt*, and elsewhere.

The Constant Bride

Do you understand the concept? The marvel? Tender at the neck,
shoulder at turn. Water freezes like this, bent and ready
to thaw. We are entering the realm of winter
but this is the exciting, awful, *now*. Remember dancing?
Audacity's threat: that it could make us fall?

Both body and soul have been sewn strict to the lining,
seam to seam. Needle curved, minuscule stitch.
Pearls furrow the bodice—hives adhered.
Then there's the bangles, the serpentine
garter wrapping the calf. O decision,

with which word will *very* now link arms?
The bridal veil drapes the bed. Worn it turns
to a rustle of besotted birds. Tonight, the mechanical
garden—the lych gate, a hinged iris. And only one wish
from which to choose: sleep and may she never wake.

The Dog Bark

Louise peered into the corner of the cabinet
of fossilized delights: mandragon manikin, a dried mermaid,

assorted dog barks of crass appetites.
It was six and dark early. Don't forget numbers, Ham said,

are only examples: one and two with their sterile marriage,
three with its tattooed face. That year the gifts were lustrous:

a bear with the head of a horse, small nipples, flowers
in its ears. Louise said, Who doesn't love

the sound of scissor snips and free-for-all terms of endearment.
The dog, they named *Lucky*

To Be Alive, and refused to let it be altered.

Louise in Love

Much had transpired in the phantom realm:
Are we whole now? Louise asked.
I think we are, the other said.

And from the mirror: no longer blue in the face, and vague;
only destiny's dove bending a broke wing and beckoning.
The ride had been open and long, the car resplendent.

What rapture, this rode into sunset. This elegant end
where a band tugs a sleeve,
a hand labors with an illusion

of waving away a thread. And then they came to something
big: down the block, winking red lights and a crowd
of compelling circumference.

They were one with the woman, her rosacea face,
the snapdragon terrier, ten men in black helmets, a man supine
on a stretcher. O the good and the evil of accident.

They were wary, and justifiably so. The mind says—*No,*
Louise admitted, but the heart, it loves repetition
and sport:

cat's paw from under the bed skirt,
dainty wile, frayed thing,
fish hook.

Like a Fire in a Fire

They were difficult to find. It was summer so
they were dust dry and sky blue. Lighter, liminal, quite likely
to follow a line completely lacking in depth.

Louise dreamed a clowder of cats was eating yesterday's dinner
of snapper and fennel. Ham dreamed a hand
was playing a tin can piano note twice too many times.

The other lay awake listening to a radio static
at the base of the stapes deep in the damaged right ear.
Soon, August would trade its heat

for September's cool shroud. The loose weave, a sieve, Louise said,
through which the tail will fall through: dysthymic October,
deathy November.

December, a drear pentimento—unveiling the mouth
at abeyance, the mind at undone. Boneheap, rock beach,
birdie girls crooning in swan-feathered caps.

O seasons, O castles, Ham said, there's still the slight flutter
of blood in an outlying vein, light trained on a landscape
of shoulder with faint smell of soap.

The Star's Whole Secret

Did she drink tea? Yes, please. And after,
the halo of a glass gone.
A taxi appeared out of elsewhere.

Five constellations, Louise said,
but only two bright stars among them. Soon, Ham said,
the whale will reach the knot of the fisherman's net;

the moon will have its face in the water.
And we'll all feel the fury of having been used
up in maelstrom and splendor.

Mother did say, Louise said, try to be popular,
pretty, and charming. Try to make others
feel clever. Without fear, what are we?

the other asked. The will, said Louise. The mill moth
and the lavish wick, breathless in the remnant
of a fire.

ERIN BELIEU

ERIN BELIEU is the author of *Infanta* (Copper Canyon Press, 1995), which was a selection of the National Poetry Series and was chosen as one of the best books of 1995 by the National Book Critics' Circle. The poems included in the anthology are from her recently published collection, *One Above and One Below* (Copper Canyon Press, 2000).

Aloyse Blair

Radio Nebraska

> If you can't be with the one you love, honey,
> Love the one you're with . . .

Good advice speaks from unlikely places, so you follow it
all along the Platte, heading west toward the panhandle,
the rumor of sand hill cranes fueling the tourist's urge,
caravans of birders cruising I-80 with a pilgrim's
progress. But what if you were born here,

and know this river's dawdle, its muddy elbows and
intentions? As a child, you had a child's frustration
with proceedings: twelve long times the hands must meet
before you reach the mountains. If you ever have a child,
remember to assure her that

one cannot really *die* of boredom, just an expression
folks use to pass the time, as one milo field drifts
into another and the same decrepit shed, year after
year, threatens to collapse. And isn't this the costume for
devotion? A sky so dense you wear the proof

of it, hostile actor in the packed cities your life is
pushing you through? An emptiness attached to
the spine like a vestigial tail? Broken Bow, Sidney, and
Alliance; Willa Cather's Red Cloud, and poor Beatrice,
her pure name made homely with the town's

local inflections. On your way through again, the cold air
puffing from the burned out thermostat barely keeps
the prairie heat at bay.

You've never seen the sand hill cranes,
but know the rites of their ethereal lovemaking.

    Otherworldly,
these alien birds, and unexpectedly beautiful.

At St. Sulpice

Because the mind is forever building its model airplane:
locust hum of colored Bakelite,

blue lobelia in a hairy root-ball, plastic bags snapping
open, and unkind

comments up from Florida, or pearl-ribbed
radicchio, purple birthmarks lolling in their bin.

For instance, Delacroix's angel at St. Sulpice
is titian-haired like Nancy Drew, fearless girl detective,

which reminds you of The (solved) Mystery
In the Golden Pavilion

and wings, of course, wings, the angel's mashed
full-nelson in the foreground under Jacob's painted weight

in a church left suspiciously unvisited by tourists
except for two,

two scholars from the Hermitage resembling Cyd Charisse
and Peter Lorre, plus one bald German,

edelweiss and Passchendaele.
Because the mind is forever building its model airplane

you have traveled off to Paris, saved up the fare
and expectations, have slept wonderfully uncomfortable

on strangely-shaped pillows
except

despite what you paid, everything resembles nothing
more than your hometown: Brigadoon

of perennial (almost eagerly) expected disappointments, as in
why have two scoops if one will do? And why have one,

etc., etc., Yours . . . sincerely, I don't believe in this
world sorrow, do you, Miss Honeychurch?

My Field Guide

Lake Pleiades, VT

I've never bothered with the names of flowers,
though now I'd like this expertise to call
them out to you as we hike in.

But I would want their true names, not
the Guide's all-classifying explanations:

for *yellow simple-shaped* or *odd-
belled purple cluster*, I'd rather plump-girl-
shaking-her-hair-out-in-the-shower,
and violet-prom-dress-circa-1960.

Or better yet, I'd have the words
that droning bee has just now written at
the throat of lakeside goldenrod. They must
be intimate—see how he calms between her?

His body, only evolution's hunt
for agitation, yet the way he gentles at
her feathered mouth. Let's call that . . . what?

Biology is obvious. Or choose
another name. No matter how you speak,
what language we might settle on,
the woodpecker won't stop her rhythmic knocking
inside the arms of tamarack,

and we've arrived at birds and bees again.
But nothing is as simple, is it?

MOLLY BENDALL

Laura Berton

MOLLY BENDALL's two collections of poems are *After Estrangement* (Peregrine Smith Books, 1992) and *Dark Summer* (Miami University Press, 1999). She teaches at the University of Southern California.

A Painter of Destinies

You said, "Come in to the light
that furs the wooden frame,
that makes the canvas porcelain."
It *is* here: the bottled music
of my likeness.
So I began to tell you how
the aromatherapy had been a failure,
but that, still, there were moments
of lucid temptations,
utterly tranquil in their strokes.
And I loved the threshold
I came to—came to dust,
the sworn chore I performed
with some panache—until my reward
was given to me
in my relatives' foreign
language, and I regressed
to loving bicycles.

But never once did I claim
settlement. Always,
I panned for topaz and took in
the unexpected visits
of music teachers, however silly
their watches were (the crystals
dramatized checkerboards and horsehair).
You've shown me the way to redo
my leaning gardens under mantles
and mutant sorrow,
grown stale in a studio like your own.
Yet after I saw the body
stripped for surgery
pining for tethered urns,
you told me, even while sitting
in the one delicate chair,
I must expect
only useless science in return.

Fete on the Lake

I hold my bet for the clouds
as our party of presumptuous boats
trembles in the changing air.
The rain hits, of course, in moments
on the overhanging branches
and sleeping birds, and stops just
as quickly, leaving our lanterns,
once intoxicants, frail flames.

Not the calmest of gatherings—
all the 8:30 fuss, the threat
of dreaming ghosts. We cheer anyway
even though our party colognes
sadden the dampness.

I'm wishing for ways to forget
your fraudulent consoling last year,
when the woman on her shallow stage
sent you into disarray . . .
She was no Scottish queen,
though I admired her martyred complexion.
You dubbed her your "sylph,"
then you were dedicated
to a pale, feathery nocturne,

and I, your devoted, tried to remember
what lightness felt like—
adrift above the weight
of gazebos and trellises—
and what stories my hats could tell.

But for now, row us gently.
Do the lake birds refuse us affectionately?

The flowery carp look panic struck
as we pass over them. Their apricot skin
is beckoning. And for a moment,
the shadowy dragonflies cast themselves
more darkly on the sky.

We disguise ourselves
with the amber-colored wine and prepare
to draw names from a glass bowl.

Watching your face lit with ribbons
of water, I say that we leave
nothing, except these tardy birds
to chance. I was afraid
I was caught in that loss once more,
when she paused hermetically
behind her playful scrim, and
I longed for trains of fruit trees
along the guilty months.

Just remind me this isn't gloom—
it's our Nile dreaming again,
and we lounge back like tired musicians
to rest our breath
while the intimate wind
invokes a little fate, rippling
like lapis lazuli—the immortal blue.

The Book of Sharp Silhouettes

Gothic flowers bedded themselves
in the edges of this night, the night
when a bullet pierced her rib precisely,
even musically, and another, her throat,
and threads of blood gathered on her blouse
into the brocade of a costume,
and she was thrown back

into a perfect arch, a balletic
plunge, her chin tilting up, until
she saw the window behind her and
in its corner the half-lit clouds
and old moon. She'd forgotten
him already—her betrayed
betrayer. He didn't know where

her gaze had traveled but jeweled eyes
had sparkled on her arms and his own
body as he noted the sequins
so purposefully arranged and sewn.
And she fell to that needle of moon
out into the woods behind her house,
where her sister took her, pulled

her away into the low-tones of dusk
to look again at the screech owl's
sculpted nest, an earth-colored pitcher,
full and comfortable at its distance,
set against the signatures of
peaks and spires—they imagined once
it held Chinese tea for them.

And this time owl was there too,
a canopy to their conversation about
leaving the stifling humidity of home,
about the poison of diamond-shaped leaves,
about the 7 p.m. freight train
that thundered miles away through the brown
petals of the canyon. Her hair

and her sister's poured down like the dark
tea of summer to meet the uneasy ferns and
torn leaves that complemented the mink wings
of the owl—its strange, aristocratic
hovering. And how the wings pursued
and interrogated, then folded
into the crackling burnt paper

of the hills behind them.
Was this lemon-eyed spy
a changeling or an interloper,
or a distraction in her own portrait
of night? It was as if the mesh of trees
had chosen her and knelt over her,
and evening's clocked arms came

to her face, then the edges of its sleeves
into her open mouth—ruthless sleeves,
like those of a queen from a story ballet
with heavy, widowy cloth.
And the sleeves reached into
her throat, past her heart,
into her voice, a voice her sister heard,

the sound that fell deeply, almost easily
until their stage was brimming
and lush, lush with the fragrance
of birds and tea that rises
on the fitful conscience of this blackened page.

DONALD BERGER

Cindy Moss

DONALD BERGER is the author of *Quality Hill* (Lost Roads Publishers, 1993). He is a lecturer and the Administrative Director of the MFA Program in Creative Writing at the University of Maryland.

The Lincoln Bedroom

I have confidence, Peacock, and my eyes are soft.
The chairs, Queen Anne, the tables of night, the beaded lamps, square
    pillows, more
symmetric than the human heart,
headboard of leaf like nothing
that can ever form.

As you love this bed it makes you think
of the other bed,
so short they had to lie him out
diagonal. The paintings of people,
ghosts coated with oil.
But then to one side
the chair of a child, who'd faced the bed
and answered questions.

Ceiling high as the thought of elephants,
great living flowers, a plate the size of a head.
Glass globes, an even ten, you can't stop counting.
Mirror, too, that doesn't reflect
so much as suck,
with curtains, metaphors for resemblance
smeared with love, a marble table,
four sad books
resting there like people
fresh out of the loveseat, pale, pretending
the rug is the sea, it looks like something strong and wet,
the bed a big black battleship, only
a hockey puck black—if only
you could catch it—this is where
I was without my normal
hesitation, almost
alone, the stomach swelling like a sponge.

"There's two of us," I wrote to myself,
afraid it might seem loud.

The Language Pile

In a language pile I should like to be starting
a language soon, a school
for after we go out
and slip on a nail
that went through and was not without
a little rust.

I had to know this
person once who couldn't speak unless he was in pain.
He kept coming back from the doctor and expecting us
to follow his idea
which was nothing more than a need that had never developed
that sense of permanent balance,
a nail passed through a hand.

Dinner in the Sun

Someone might think that because New Jersey is a relatively easy concept
Of the author, its characters too charged with the beach and its words nasty
    and pelletlike,
Instead of building on their own a passion for complex fully developed human
    beings—
Do you think the decision is accurate?
Is the boy merely representing degrees of calm?
Which characters are more or less openly smooth, or square?

Does anyone guess that God is simply turning coldly away
Or crouched in the basement in front of his workbench
In favor of loving a cigar?
Does Denny (the brother) ever seem torn by loving his shortcuts?
Does Harta, his mom, ever seem more horn-haired than her son?
If it's true, does someone think the author wanted us to feel all this, or do we
    respond to the characters
Distantly now that they're gathered into a headlock?

"I thought everything about grown-up life was like furniture," Max, the father,
    tells his son, "solid, heavy, and forever and ever . . .
Hoo-boy, was I wrong," he says. Needing this book in the late
Twentieth century, when we forget how hot it gets, does the narrator's
    spywork, his look at himself, seem coupled properly with the right
    moment?
Does anyone think the boy is oblivious as much to his robin's egg blue as he is
    the neon heat of his adjective?
To powerful chitterings of waters in general?

The Jersey men discuss Minkoff, the doc, pages before the reader actually sees
    him raise his hands, then put a fist in front of his mouth.
Why does someone sense God chose to wobble, notebook in hand?
What do Denny and Derwent's reactions to Jersey show us about their surveil-
    lance emplacements, about their mail, delivered by someone who seemed to
    float?

Before his rays of light are removed from him, does Denny resort to the voice
    of a wounded animal?

Is he a muscular character? Does his wind not touch itself with a fist?
How does the author peer through the hole?
What does Denny's opinion of danger—that he enjoys it for its "splinters of
wood whittled into likenesses of long-faced men"—eventually do for him?
At the center of the book once the boy's force is ultimate, does Denny seem in
any way a familiar thick feeling?

God himself rarely stirs, but the author wiggles his ears with a silvery laugh.
What does anyone guess the book is saying about the brother's radiating out-
ward, while cutting towards mirrors?
How do the stems of the boy, Harta, Max and Denny reflect (refract?) on the
burning cone?
Would God have considered it a happy ending for Denny if, as begun at the
end, Sabina had laughed and started lifting him?
Of if she had ended up laughing indefinitely, and still "extending a long finger
at the carrot sticks," as she'd always done, before being chosen to live in this
particular spot?

"I sat up in bed," Denny says to us at one point. "I want to go on the planes,"
says the boy. "They go up and up and up."
What is the relationship between sleep and flight in these pages?
Has the relationship between sleep and flight changed in today's sunburst of
reds?
"The wind is clean," the narrator says at one point.
How often does the wind enjoy the nubbly feeling of these characters?

The book THE BOY began its life as an expression of divine mildness.
What part do the eyes play in the whiteness of the story, on the translucency of
the islands of the characters?
What does anyone think the author did by ending that he couldn't have had he
left the book with the rest of his mind?

DAVID BIESPIEL

Tricia Snell

DAVID BIESPIEL was born in Tulsa, Oklahoma, in 1964 and grew up in Texas. He attended Boston University on a diving scholarship and later studied and taught at the University of Maryland and at Stanford. A recipient of NEA and Stegner fellowships, he currently lives in Oregon, where he develops Junior Olympic divers and directs The Attic. Biespiel's first volume of poems is *Shattering Air* (BOA Editions, 1996).

Tower

Fifteen years old and naked, quivering,
Stomachs flat on the ten-meter platform
Of a strange pool, 3 o'clock in the morning,
Bonnie Horton and I leaned our heads over
The hard edge of the tower to make out
The liquid surface below us, four arms
Hanging limp, loose, in the 90-degree
Darkness, swaying, knocking each other,
Playfully pulling a wrist hard enough
So one of us would fall into the flat
Blue hole of relief. I kept looking
For the water's wind-ripple, but so dark,
We could barely see the starting blocks
Or the deck chairs. And I could hardly see
The fence we'd snuck over, to climb up, strip
For the first time together, kiss, and touch
Helplessly, hysterically, Bonnie's two
Gold bracelets jingling like laughter,
Not a care but to hold her body

As close to mine as she'd allow,
To reverse-somersault down finally
To cool off. I never wanted to leave
That tower, never wanted to let go
Of a moment that lucky, but suddenly,
In the play and tug, one of her bracelets
Broke—I tried to watch it plummet,
See the splash, jump down to get it.
I couldn't. It bounced. Clink-clink-
Clink on the concrete bottom of the well.
We lay there disordered,
The air rough and shattering, distance
Clenched in our lungs like a giant fist,
The heat lingering. Bonnie said, *O*, or cried,
Softly, I don't remember. Amazed,
I was looking at my hands, and I still wonder
How they could hold pleasure one minute, close
To the lips, touching, wet. Skinless wind
The next. The veins throbbing over the cold depths
As they would the next morning at ten-meter
Workout, at our pool, before my first dive,
A front one-and-one-half with a full twist,
My body tearing the sky, the cool water
Pure, fragrant, taking me whole.

After the Wedding

I hear the wood slats wince on the back porch
And leap at the spruce bough's mid-evening bend,
The way I heard it weeping during the vows
While a cardinal jumped from spruce to pine,
Settled for a low branch in the day's union,
Its backswept crest like a four-corner fold,
The sharp conical bill hard as a nut cracker.
Its ethnic, muscular black fell across the face
Like the wind's brush on the air through the looped
Crest and spindle gaps on the rocker. Then gone

Without a whistle. Then the sway,
The long wooden pulse and throb, the rutted
Boards' plumage hard as wind under the wing.

Under a Blossoming Plum Tree

Labor Day, 1996

Under a blossoming plum tree
In a summer of peace,
Tallying the steps

The gang of jays made near the blackberry-
Entangled roses, I thought of the glassy
Distance between loved ones—

A river without a bridge,
Dying lilacs
In the merlot bottle.

      *   *   *

What the Earth means—
The dirty crabapple leans down

Crippled more
Than a windblown candle.

Like murmuring
Old men

Fearlessly bowing
Their heads

To the eternal flame,
The apples keep falling

Bruised for weeks
In the humid grass.

*   *   *

Once waking at night
My lover beside me,
I watched the slick grass
Sputter: The heart's like that—
A wick in a drafty window.
                I'd awakened
From a dream
Of a black room
Filling with water.
My lover beside me,
Her eyes like chicory.
She was swimming
In and out of
The tumbling waves,
Turning her head
To open her mouth
To the actual air.

*   *   *

Inside a vinegar bottle
Is the Caribbean.
When I turn the glass
Upside down
The imprisoned sea
Tumbles, pounds,
                and settles
Like dust.

*   *   *

Plum trees, light a dazzle,
The crabapples thudding
Without replica
One by one
Onto the grass.

*   *   *

When I hold the ocean
In a bottle sideways

The bubbled air
Stops still:

This day, the next,
The purpose,

The work,
Is language.

*   *   *

What if Uncle Reuben hadn't said a week before his 97th birthday
That he didn't believe in God, because where was God
When the Jews were holding their six million last breaths,
And I said, how do you account for it not being seven million, fifteen million,
    fifty million?

*   *   *

Beyond us
There's a spatter
Of stars
And, what,
Something better
Than Earth?

RICHARD BLANCO

Carlos Betancourt

RICHARD BLANCO was made in Cuba, assembled in Spain, and imported to the United States, where he was raised and educated in Miami. His first book of poetry is *City of a Hundred Fires*, winner of the 1997 Agnes Starrett Prize (University of Pittsburgh Press, 1998). A builder of bridges and poems, Blanco received a BS in civil engineering and an MFA from Florida International University. He teaches at Central Connecticut State University.

Last Night in Havana

Drifting from above, the palms seem to sink
willingly into the saffron ground, all I can map
is the marble veins of rivers turning static,
the island coastline retreating like a hem
from the sargasso patches of Caribbean.
I think of you *primo*, huddled on the edge
of an Almendares curb last night,
El Greco shadow spilt across the street,
and over the tracks stapled to the weeds
below your open bedroom window.
Covered in cobwebs of humid wind,
we slapped at unreachable mosquitos
as Havana's tenements collapsed around us,
enclosed us like the yellow of old books
or the stucco walls of a hollow chapel.
You confessed you live ankled in the sand
of a revolution, watching an unparted sea,
marking tides and learning currents
that will carry you through the straits

to my door, blistered and salted, but alive.
You said you want silence, you want to leave
the sweep of the labor trains in your window,
the creak of your father's wheelchair in the hall
searching for a bottle of pills he will find empty,
and the slam of your eyelids forcing sleep.
The tires are ready, bound with piano wire,
the sail will be complete with the linen scraps
your mother will stitch together after midnights
when the neighbors are trying to fall asleep.
Last night in Havana, your face against your knees,
your words drowning with the lees in an empty bottle
of bootleg wine you clutched around the neck
and will keep to store fresh water.

Letter to El Flaco on His Birthday

Querido Flaco,

The ride was cool, wasn't it? Us five
modern Spartans on a rampage in Zamar's '67 Olds,
heavy solid steel doors that slammed like traps,
neat triangular window slits drawing in the rushing wind,
a new paint job the color of a clear-blue breath mint,
itchy foam oozing from gashed seats,
the smell of monoxides and cigarettes
as familiar and engulfing as memories of fathers
and Saturday mornings spent learning how to drive.
We've learned how to drive, we've driven:
to work where we park our lives behind mahogany,
to classroom ideals or to nickel-beer joints;
through stokes of rain and the warping light
of unattempted allies that swallow city rapture
the way black holes take in starlight.
All those miles. All the books we've read—
of poetry and philosophy, of art and architecture—
and still we can't decide whether to burn recklessly
or become simple verses of ethics and obligation.

Today, the road led to the Pink Pussycat,
we strapped dollar bills in the lace garters
of our mothers and our sisters (not-dancing),
of our future wives and unborn daughters (not-dancing),
wiggling around brass posts like licorice,
as we stood ready to evaporate in the heat
of the flashing bulbs that trimmed the stage.
Did you think of da Vinci or Dante, did you decide
between glances at Rita's brown-nippled breasts
jelloing side-to-side above the mirrored stool. Don't.
Instead, count the sprinkled late night drives, the road
a slippery winding of eel skin, reflecting, if not stars,
the equally spaced cinnamon haloes of luminaries
guiding you home to those empty rooms you fill
with the pulse of *bembés* pulled from Tito's bongo,
the African gods hibernating in your black forest eyelashes,
the heartfuls of musical orgy from Mulata's studio
where you've thrown off your suede bucks
and learned how to dance like a Salsa King,
in the stairwell of a four-story walk-up.

Don't think of Nietzsche or Eliot. Don't decide.
Today think of the finite number of midnight runs
for pizza or nachos, drive-thrus and one last smoke;
the times you fill the gas tank for the ride home,
the traffic lights stop flashing, begin their steady burn,
and the night closes a cappella in a song all our own.

Shaving

I am not shaving, I'm writing about it.
And I conjure the most elaborate idea—
how my beard is a creation of silent labor
like ocean steam rising to form clouds,
or the bloom of spiderwebs each morning;
the discrete mystery of how whiskers grow,
like the drink roses take from the vase,

or the fall of fresh rain, becoming
a river, and then rain again, so silently.
I think of all these slow and silent forces
and how quietly my father's life passed us by.

I think of those mornings, when I *am* shaving,
and remember him in a masquerade of foam, then,
as if it was his beard I took the blade to,
the memory of him in tiny snips of black whiskers
swirling in the drain—dead pieces of the self
from the face that never taught me how to shave.
His legacy of whiskers that grow like black seeds
sown over my cheek and chin, my own flesh.

I am not shaving, but I will tell you about the mornings
with a full beard and the blade in my hand,
when my eyes don't recognize themselves
in a mirror echoed with a hundred faces
I have washed and shaved—it is in that split second,
when perhaps the roses drink and the clouds form,
when perhaps the spider spins and rain transforms,
that I most understand the invisibility of life
and the intensity of vanishing, like steam
at the slick edges of the mirror, without a trace.

The Silver Sands

Before the revival of quartz pinks and icy blues
on this neon beach of Art Deco hotels and boutiques,
there were the twilight verandas lined with retirees,
the cataract eyes of Mrs. Stein who would take us
for mezzanine bingo and pancakes at Wolfies;
I remember her beautiful orthopedic wobble.

Before sequined starlets popping out of limousine doors
and booze on the breath of every glitter-paved street,
there were the five-year-old summers of flamingo towels,
transistor radios blaring something in Spanish we ignored,
only curious of driftwood, washed-up starfish and jellyfish,
the beauty of broken conchs and our moated sand castles.

Before the widened sidewalks and pretentious cafés
where I take my cappuccino sprinkled with cinnamon,
our mothers were peacocks in flowered bathing caps
posing for sandy Polaroids like pageant contestants;
there were fifteen-cent Cokes to their ruby lips
and there was nothing their beauty couldn't conquer.

Before the demolition of the Silver Sands Hotel,
our fathers spun dominos under the thatch-palm gazebos,
drank then insulted the scenery: *Nada like our Varadero,*
there the sand was powder; the water truly aquamarine.
I remember the poor magic of those voices—
how beautifully they remembered beauty.

Tía Olivia Serves Wallace Stevens a Cuban Egg

The ration books voided, there was little to eat,
so Tía Olivia ruffled four hens to serve Stevens
a fresh *criollo* egg. The singular image lay limp,
floating in a circle of miniature roses and vines
etched around the edges of the rough dish.
The saffron, inhuman soul staring at Stevens
who asks what yolk is this, so odd a yellow?

Tell me Señora, if you know, he petitions,
what exactly is the color of this temptation:
I can see a sun, but it is not the color of suns
nor of sunflowers, nor the yellows of Van Gogh,
it is neither corn nor school pencil, as it is,
so few things are yellow, this, even more precise.

He shakes some salt, eye to eye hypothesizing:
a carnival of hues under the gossamer membrane,
a liqueur of convoluted colors, quarter-part orange,
imbued shadows, watercolors running a song
down the spine of praying stems, but what, then,
of the color of the stems, what green for the leaves,
what color the flowers; what of order for our eyes
if I can not name this elusive yellow, Señora?

Intolerant, Tía Olivia bursts open Stevens's yolk,
plunging into it with a sharp piece of Cuban toast:
It is yellow, she says, *amarillo y nada más, bien?*
The unleased pigments begin to fill the plate,
overflow onto the embroidered place mats,
stream down the table and through the living room
setting all the rocking chairs in motion then
over the mill tracks cutting through cane fields,
a viscous mass downing palm trees and shacks.

In its frothy wake whole choirs of church ladies
clutch their rosary beads and sing out in Latin,
exhausted *macheteros* wade in the stream,
holding glinting machetes overhead with one arm;
cafeteras, '57 Chevys, uniforms and empty bottles,
mangy dogs and fattened pigs saved from slaughter,
Soviet jeeps, *Bohemia* magazines, park benches,
all carried in the egg lava carving the molested valley
and emptying into the sea. *Yellow*, Stevens relents,
Yes. But then what the color of the sea, Señora?

NICK CARBÓ

Denise Duhamel

NICK CARBÓ, a Spanish citizen, was born (1964) and raised in the Philippines. He is a winner of an NEA Fellowship in Poetry (1997), NYFA Fellowship in Poetry (1999), and is the author of *El Grupo McDonald's* (Tia Chucha Press, 1996). Carbó is the editor of *Returning a Borrowed Tongue* (Coffeehouse Press, 1996) and *The Other Half of the Sky* (2000).

I Found Orpheus Levitating

above the hood of an illegally parked red Toyota Corolla
on Mabini Street. He was tired of all that descending
into and ascending from those pretentious
New Yorker and *Atlantic Monthly* poems.
He asked me to give him new clothes so I dressed him
in an old barong tagalog and some black pants.
Because he wanted new friends in a new land, I introduced
him to Kapitan Kidlat, our local comic book hero.
But after a few whips of that lightning bolt, Orpheus
recognized Kidlat as Zeus in another clever disguise.
So, I took him to Mt. Makiling where Malakas & Maganda
(the mythical first Filipino man and woman) live
in a mansion with an Olympic-size swimming pool.
He said Maganda's aquiline features remind him
of Eurydice and Malakas has the solid torso
of a younger Apollo. He asked me to translate
the word, *threesome* into Tagalog.
Malakas & Maganda agreed and they stripped

Orpheus of his clothes as they led him
to their giant bamboo bed.
I waited outside in the car all afternoon before he emerged
from the mansion smelling of Sampaguitas and Ylang-Ylang.
He was hungry so we drove to the nearest
Kamayan restaurant where he learned
how to eat rice and pork abobo with his bare hands.
"It's wonderful! This was the way it used to be.
When the industrial revolution happened, all of us on Mt. Olympus
suddenly had forks and knives appear in our hands. We used
them as garden tools at first." Afterwards, he wanted to drink
and go dancing. I paid the hundred-peso cover charge
for both of us at the Hobbit House in Ermita. The first
thing he did in the dark, smoky bar was trip over
one of the dwarf waiters, all the waiters were dwarfs. *"I'm sorry,*
I couldn't see. It feels as if I had just walked into a Fellini film."
He placed his hands in front of him as if he were pushing
back a glass wall. *"No, No, I'm not in a movie,*
I'm inside a fucking poem!
I can see the poet's scrunched-up face on the other side
of the computer screen!" I told Orpheus to shut up
or the bouncers, who were not the same size as the waiters,
would throw us out of the bar. We sat
in a booth across from each other and ordered double
shots of Tanduay Rum. I asked him if he understood
the concept of "the willing suspension of disbelief."
I asked him to look me straight
in the face before he ran out into the street.

Robo

> "Was Andalusia here or there? On the land . . . or in the poem?"
> —Mahmoud Darwish

I must admit to this outright theft.
Before the crickets could impede me,

I reached outside my window
to grab as much of Andalusia as

I could in the palm of my hand.
I took the evening's silver

from the olive trees, the yellow slumber
from the lemons, the recipe for *gazpacho.*

I made a small incision in my heart
and slipped in as much as my left

and right ventricles could hold.
I reached for a pen and a piece of paper

to ease-out the land into this poem.
I closed the small incision in my heart

and closed the wooden shutters
of my window.

Verso Libre

In this white room in Mojácar,
I wait for the potato of tears

that will arrive in an ordinary
wheel barrow when news

of the death of a family member
spurts through the phone. Five-thirty

and the Andalusian cocks begin
their newspaper routes.

I can read all the signs—
the odor of disturbing dreams,

the umber-spotted lizard on the wall,
the sound of the waning moon.

I have to write it all down.
in this white room in Mojácar.

ANNE CASTON

ANNE CASTON is the author of *Flying Out With the Wounded*, which won the 1996 New York University Press Prize for Poetry. A graduate of the Warren Wilson MFA Program for Writers, and a former Jenny McKean Moore Writer-in-Washington at the George Washington University, she is currently an assistant professor of English at the University of Alaska.

The Burden

By the time I got to them, the woman was stoned
    on sorrow and half a jar of gin; her man,
cold sober, was praying and casting out demons.
    On the kitchen table, a box: a doll
dressed for burial. On the ashy hearth nearby, the dead
    child, swaddled in a filthy towel.

I stooped to see: again, a son,
    third one in three years to arrive half-made.
A changeling, the man called it, *the Devil's*
    work in a woman's womb. He left off
the exorcism of her body long enough
    to tell me: *Throw it, like the others, to the dogs.*

They'll not touch the body again, not even
    to dispose of it; that's why I'm called, three times now.
No sin for me to lift the damaged and dead.
    Lord knows, I've done worse. So I folded the boy
back into his rags and left with him
    slung in the crook of my arm.

I threw the dogs, starved as they were, the blood-caked
    afterbirth and cord, then drove seven miles west
to a rotting trestle hung out over a gorge.
    I slid down the mud-slick slope to the swollen
bank of the creek and pulled back the reeking rags
    to have, in the bright morning light, a better look.

I tell you, it shook me a little, the sight:

the translucent fetal skin, all the veins
    visible and cursive like something penned
in an indecipherable hand, and under the milky lids, two
    yellow orbs—no pupils, no irises. Ten fingers; ten toes.
And when I rolled him over, near the base of the skull,
    the blue-gray brain bulged free.

Worse yet: all was rot and ooze
    down the underbelly and along the swollen sex.
When I stooped to the shallows, to rinse the body
    of birth's debris, some of the skin washed
free of the bones; I lifted what was left of the boy
    and lay him down in the dew-drenched grass.

I tore the ruined linen three times down its length,
    knotted the ends together, and wound it, whole-cloth,
'round the body, head to toe, binding a stone in as I went.
    I tied it off with a double knot, breathed
a blessing over it, and cast the bundle into the stream:
    it bobbed twice and went under; it surfaced again.

Then it sank and was gone for good.

In this is the burden of lifting to light
    from the squalor of this world
what is—or is almost—undone:
    that a straw doll can be blessed and laid to rest
under a white-washed cross on which is carved *Boy Tolbertson*,
    while the syphilitic's son drifts—as he has now

for twenty-two years—through the dream-riddled nights
    of the rest of my life, a changeling, wrapped
in the sins of his father, in his milky skin
    and his rough-knotted shroud, moving beyond
minnows and old moorings and my meager blessing
    towards the sea and his other lost brothers.

Blowing Eggs

My grandmother taught me the delicate trick:
to choose a silver pin, to prick
both ends, to put the mouth to it, just so,
to blow until the insides are blown clear.

What's left in hand is brittle, but more
amenable to art, to the swab and splash of color,
the varnish, the slick veneer.

A thing like that could last for years
on some high shelf, outlive the daily scramble
common things will come to in the end.

And the hen who laid the egg?
My brother and I, in mischief, once slipped
the painted thing beneath her in the nest;
she shrieked and pecked it to bits.

Gathering at the River

I.

In a thicket this morning, river-hung, a feed sack;
in it, a millstone and twelve gray kittens.

I have loved this river all my life. Also the God
who, surely, looked on and did nothing.

II.

My father says God is The Potter
who sets each man, as clay, on a wheel,

and makes of him a vessel, which He then perfects
in the great fires of tribulation.

If the firing is done well, that man will endure,
and his faith, as the saints before him endured

their stonings, drownings, boilings-in-oil.
Like in the Book of Martyrs which I saw once as a child:

the righteous in white robes who, though demons gnashed at them,
lifted their eyes to heaven and praised God.

God will, in His own time—so says my father—deliver them.
Joy cometh in the morning.

III.

Shall we gather at the river, the old hymn goes, *gather
with the saints at the river that flows by the throne of God.*

But this river runs to sea and I am no saint this morning,
something in me drowned as these twelve dead

disciples of the sack, drowned
beyond praising anything.

IV.

Potter, after the wheel and the fire of this life,
You can cast me off on the banks of this river, a half-wrought

vessel, flawed: a busted cup where the dead are hung, a music
You'll hear again when the wind goes, singing, through it.

A.V. CHRISTIE

A. V. CHRISTIE's first book of poems, *Nine Skies* (University of Illinois Press), appeared in the National Poetry Series in 1996, as selected by Sandra McPherson. She holds degrees from Vassar College and the University of Maryland. Recently, she's been Visiting Poet at Villanova University and Bryn Mawr College. She lives in Malvern, Pennsylvania.

The Hollywood Finch

I thought someone had said Olmsted brought them
east to brighten the edge, finish
with a peripheral and brief red
his Central Park. But here, a few pages past
the Ash-throated Flycatcher, Dark-eyed
Junco, I read of the modest and ruddy House Finch
whom California cage-bird dealers dubbed
"Hollywood" and, in 1940, shipped in a purplish,
illegal scheme to New York. Fearing violations,
fines, the store clerks of Manhattan
released the birds which spread to Long Island
survived north to Connecticut and south
to Maryland where this morning I watched them
flicking suet in the angled sun. And I thought
to myself in the early hush—how tenuous
and grandiose are the plans, how small
these beaks eating the seed of the brittlebush.

Overture

for Gabriella

There had been a cricket in the basement
when I dreamt you were an unopened envelope on my chest.
I heard on the radio how silverware suddenly tarnishes in a drawer
before disaster, tornadoes, sudden changes in weather.
The voice on the radio, on the lookout, she said, "It's beautiful . . .
it's not dark . . . it's good." Meaning the silverware.

For weeks we watched your heart
your breath, dip and peak and wander along the screen.
The week we brought you home, they found the long-gone
missing woman's body while deerhunting in one of the western
counties under the year's first snow
         —every valley shall be exalted.

The television vet spoke of the jealous dog
swallowing all of its owner's jewelry whenever she left,
even the dreamed-after diamond tennis bracelet.
I saw a bee-bearded man, listened to Tchaikovsky's span of months
and to a piece of music called the "Silken Ladder Overture,"

and just as finely were we ascending to some place past
the blurred coming-home-from-the-hospital photograph, beyond
even sight of our selves. I dreamt someone asked
for a lock of *my* hair in a world of perfectly
cloned sheep, of "silver needles" tea beneath

the all-throated prize finches. A blood and primrose world—
my darling—a white-tea-of-leaf-buds world, mild as your first tears.
When you sleep beside me, my arm locks across you.
Oh, how we'll whirl and circle, be whirled and fear-throated
a breathless carnivalesque, a ride of spinning-cups.

Coming Off a Depression, She Prepares for Venice

I am tempted by rumors, by history,
today reading Sarpi who here mapped the contraction
of the iris, believed the very air
was predatory. I almost respond
to the mosaic's precision, to every last inch
of gilding—like the yearned-for drink.
I feel the stones of Venice sinking.
I picture the monk hung in a cage, in an air
riddled with midnight bells from the Campanile.
Another spectacle for the sightseer
in a Piazza already thick with jugglers and lace.

But one storey up from this
pillaged booty is the luring beauty—
like a sickness, the real story.
I fold the page down and return:
There, on the signora's table
a blue-and-white china bowl, ten-lire pieces
in the bottom and clean water in which swim
two languid goldfish, all color spent
in them. From time to time the signora drops
a fresh coin in, and they are fed
on the chemical reaction, or so she believes.
They barely live on this, live on in this
sad fountain, on the shine of their coins.

Certainly, I see how they are the workings
out of my own reflection. But to me
they are also a sort of perfection.
And although the domes and gondolas,
the grandeur and blandishments of all Venice
beckon, Titian's own luxuriant incarnadine
alight in the inclined forehead, the dreaminess
of each back street—sunning finches
and windowboxes—I am drawn back, claimed.

The Possible Man

for Vic Fitterman
and for my sister on her wedding day

For years the drops of belladonna in our eyes,
pupils wide, poison-wide with devotion.

We lived on a black acre changing hands
in a room which seemed to say, "my love
is here" or "my love has just left."

And the aphrodisiac eels astir
in the bathtub, the dove's brains, fennel,
a musky glass of cognac.
We were the nightly part of a dictatorship.

When he sat slicing oranges, revealing
the hidden system, one after another, intricate
glistenings, eight and ten oranges, pure wet
color in a bowl, we said to ourselves
"he is a genius"—
                    in our confusion
we said it again when he ate them—juice
running, rinds like paper boats on the carpet
all as he pictured us,
the wide open white plywood bodies
on the firing range
and all of that shining blood.

Do we ever truly escape, then,
to this lazy stroll through the Luxembourg Gardens
its sweet boredom of forget-me-nots,
small sailboats and fountain,
to the plainest of moments
with our husbands?
        In sleep we hear them—
our possible men—"that's right,"
"that's right" is all that they say.

And when will they call our names,
the new name, enticing us away
from a beautiful terror?

LESLEY DAUER

Arthur Dauer

LESLEY DAUER's poetry has appeared in a number of journals, including *New England Review, Poetry,* and *Seneca Review.* Her first book of poems, *The Fragile City* (Bluestem Press, 1996), won the Bluestem Award. She teaches at Foothill College in Los Altos Hills, California.

Falling

You're pressing your fingers against the sky,
asking Jesus if he sees how close those trees are.
You don't believe in Jesus. A stewardess takes everything
sharp that could hurt you: plastic cups, prayer beads.
All of her omelets are gone. You're watching your window
like television—a show about the suburbs, those stubborn lives.
Whole families relax and look lovely at home.
You're folding your hands around the armrests,
feeling the vague sadness of the stewardess' voice.
There are no clouds today above the boxwoods.
You could live in a world so solidly blue.

Mammals

As soon as I left,
my friends had an orgy.

Lemurs look down
from the trees.

I'm not a very naked person.

Some astronauts fear loneliness
more than physical danger.

I'm further from earth
than I wanted to be.

Rarely terrestrial,
lemurs live in Madagascar.

Evolution is our working thumbs.

Warm animals curl into each other,
often, quite easily.

The 20th Century

Long after the time we were supposed to arrive,
our bus is submerged and full of water.

No longer luggage, sweaters and skirts take new shape,
float to the surface as jellyfish.

The rescue workers would like to soothe you,
but they'd be wrong to—

look at our clothes, abandoned and bloated.
There was always something overwhelmed about us.

Suddenly ancient, we're simply your gargoyle friends:
stone faces in a row behind safety windows,

white and round as babies. Evolution involves crawling
from the water. We were only here for a tour.

The Woman in the Film

Because the film is running backwards,
a fireman carries a woman up his ladder
and places her gently in a burning building.
She curls softly between her bed sheets
just as a slight line of smoke
winds around the room. I feel I should say something
to the projectionist—I begin to think backwards
to my childhood, when I lit matches
and threw them over the fence.
A fireman shows me what might have burned
besides the toolshed. He motions his hand
towards my family, until my mother tells him to stop.
I head to the projectionist's booth.
On screen, the fire's receding
towards the back of the woman's house—
my mind rewinds further until I'm nothing
but a look Father gives to Mother over a candle
in some restaurant, and further still,
until my parents haven't met.
The projectionist doesn't hear me knocking.
The audience is laughing. I turn to find the fire's
gone out by itself, and the woman's own child
has just put a match back into its box.

OLENA KALYTIAK DAVIS

James J. Davis

OLENA KALYTIAK DAVIS is the author of *And Her Soul Out Of Nothing* (University of Wisconsin Press, 1997), winner of the 1997 Brittingham Prize. The recipient of a Rona Jaffe Foundation Writers Award, she lives in San Francisco.

In the Clear Long After

Spring is cheap, but clean of sky. Long after she used to
meet him on the sly. He didn't say much, because to
speak you need a voice, need lead. Among the dead there were
such fresh ghosts, they were still breathing. Through their
mouths. Time, time, to adjust to an other. An ether
O so—No—too sweet. Intox-icated with permeability. 'Tis nox-
ious, to eat evanescence. However steadily, however slowly.
They stemmed into heady blows.
They missed
the stain. Of blue berries and argument. They missed
their lips. The yew and the thorns. They missed.
Their flaws.

O, to be stung by an errant bee. O, to sting.
O, to see you again. Covered in spring.

A New Philosophy of Composition, or, How to Ignore the Non-Reasoning Creature Capable of *Speeech* Perched Outside Your Bathroom Window

It was bleak december just last night or the night
just before-*Pravda*! I mean, *It's true!*-like Prado says: god
had taken poetry away from you: a stone
was just a stone. But today today today everything
is pinioned, laced, and *fuck me!*, new: this crazy purple
toothbrush afloat in the complicated trash, that
strange yellow bird over there, and the blue-green sash
that hangs in the rosepale sky speaks to you-*o.k., o.k.,*
I mean, to me: each word, like, say, *cor-bi-ere* and *la-for-*
gue means something more than it used to-did, did! gather
gather gather and round because today I'm made
of sacred ground everything plants itself inside me grows
(I know now what was missing then I know now what was
present then it was moving it was still but I couldn't see
within) now now now it stops and spires, now now now
it rolls and gyres-*Yeats!*: here all the barrel-hops are knit
here all the serpent-tails are bit here all the gyres converge
in one . . . I meant: *Yikes!* and, no, I'm not done-a fire *is*
in me head! I'm in the *zone!*: in Marseilles among the wa-
termelons in Coblentz at the Giant's Hostelry in
Rome under a Japanese medlar-tree! Surely, surely
it's the second coming! ". . . or *the third*", broke in who 'til then
seemed like such a sweet and mellow bird, under his beak, but
I heard him, I heard him . . . W*hat matter!* The rhythm
finds me rinds me books open brooks open too I have eur-
asian steps matches tipped-blue that light on anything
everywhere I'm a live a fire a flame in this morning
light I'm far more bright than must be right. I can hear
the defunctive music! I can glean and gleam and brew
today I believe I might be able to do
what was once to me assigned years ago and *you're right!*
only last last last lastnight! Finally! dickinson's
and modigliani's sex exposed Finally! I can
see the foreign clocks the feather beds the eider-
down and the long white cocks fish that swim and open letters

to boot sweaters warm again! *"The worst are filled with*
passionate intensity—" Warned again! by that
unseemly but seemingly-well-educated bird
as if on cue, but, hey, I shot right back: *take thy beak*
from out my heart, said I, 'cause, like, *What matter!* These
photos once framed now cough and sneeze this pen rights it-
self flows with ease and I can feel the trees remember
their long lost leaves-*o.k., o.k* so the dogs bark
as they have barked and barked before but the road came by
and drove me out to shore sails set sail and pails fill up with
sand lovers dress set out for land berrigan marries not-
ley again! and again! again my husband dawns a new
hand sown and flowered shirt I weigh much much less today and
more and more I float above the moat full of serpents beasts
and other fiendly things the castle sways the horses take
on wings "*. . . And Philomel becometh dumb*"- but O! not you
bleak-beak-ed burd-en-*o.k. o.k.*, Quoth I: *What-ever!*
Who cares if you laugh as you have laughed and laughed before,
behind my back when I was just a somber bore, a strag-
gler headed east, then west, with a pocket full of seeds
and subway tokens, a cracked tooth, a *Damn!*, a broken
nail. Bitten, bitter, lit! Forsooth and forsaken! *Lo!* I
travelled but it wouldn't travel me, I smoked and turned to
greying smoke, I listened to all they had to say-felt *dick-*
turns out I held it in until today! *Sacre-Coeur!*
Today I am so found I am newly lost. *Vallejo!*
I mean: *Way-to-go!* What happens next happens now! Today
I have drunk the stone and I will carry it with me, for
a short long luminous while.

A Small Number

So far, have managed, Not
Much. So far, a few fractures, a few factions, a Few
Friends. So far, a husband, a husbandry, Nothing
Too complex, so far, followed the Simple
Instructions. Read them twice. So far, memorized three Moments,

Buried a couple deaths, those turning faces. So far, two or Three
Sonnets. So far, some berrigan and Some
Keats. So far, a scanty list. So far, a dark wood. So far, Anti-
Thesis and then, maybe, a little thesis. So far, a small Number
Of emily's letters. So far, tim not dead. So far, Matt
Not dead. So far, jim. So far, Love
And love, not so far. Not so love. So far, no-Hope.
So far, all face. So far, scrapped and scraped, but Not
With grace. So far, not Very.

Sweet Reader, Flanneled and Tulled

Reader unmov'd and Reader unshaken, Reader unsedc'd
and unterrified, through the long-loud and the sweet-still
I creep toward you. Toward you, I thistle and I climb.

I crawl, Reader, servile and cervine, through this blank
season, counting—I sleep and I sleep. I sleep,
Reader, toward you, loud as a cloud and deaf, Reader, deaf

as a leaf. Reader: *Why don't you turn
pale?* and, *Why don't you tremble?* Jaded, staid
Reader, You—who can read this and not even

flinch. Bare-faced, flint-hearted, recoilless
Reader, dare you—Rare Reader, listen
and be convinced: Soon, Reader,

soon you will leave me, for an italian mistress:
for her dark hair, and her moon-lit
teeth. For her leopardi and her cavalcanti,

for her lips and clavicles; for what you want
to eat, eat, eat. Art-lover, rector, docent!
Do I smile? I, too, once had a brash artless

feeder: his eye set firm on my slackening
sky. He was true! He was thief! In the celestial sense
he provided some, some, some

(much-needed) relief. Reader, much-slept with and Reader, I will die
without touching, You, Reader, You: mr. small-
weed, mr. broad-cloth, mr. long-dark-day. And the italian mis-

fortune you will heave me for, for
her dark hair and her moonlit-teeth. You will love her well in-
to three-or-four cities, and then, you will slowly

sink. Reader, I will never forgive you, but not, poor
cock-sure Reader, not, for what you think. O, Reader
Sweet! and Reader Strange! Reader Deaf and Reader

Dear, I understand youyourself may be hard-
pressed to bare this small and un-necessary burden
having only just recently gotten over the clean clean heart-

break of spring. And I, Reader, I am but the daughter
of a tinker. I am not above the use of bucktail spinners,
white grubs, minnow tails, Reader, worms

and sinkers. Thisandthese curtail me
to be brief: Reader, our sex gone
to wildweather. YesReaderYes—that feels much-much

better. (And my new Reader will come to me empty-
handed, with a countenance that roses, lavenders, and cakes.
And my new Reader will be only mildly disappointed.

My new Reader can wait, can wait, can wait.) Light-
minded, snow-blind, nervous, Reader, Reader, troubled, Reader,
what d'ye lack? Importunate, unfortunate, Reader:

You are cold. You are sick. You are silly.
Forgive me, kind Reader, forgive me, I had not intended to step this quickly
    this far
back. Reader, we had a quiet wedding: he&I, theparson

&theclerk. Would I could, stead-fast, gracilefacile Reader! Last,
good Reader, tarry with me, jessa-mine Reader. Dar-
(jee)ling, bide! Bide, Reader, tired, and stay, stay, stray Reader,

true. *R.: I had been secretly hoping this would turn into a love
poem.* Disconsolate. Illiterate. Reader,
I have cleared this space for you, for you, for you.

DEBRA KANG DEAN

DEBRA KANG DEAN was born in 1955 in Honolulu, Hawaii. She has published two collections of poetry: *Back to Back* (1997), which won the Harperprints Poetry Chapbook Competition, and *News of Home* (1998), the nineteenth volume in BOA Editions' A. Poulin, Jr., New Poets of America Series. A contributing editor for *Tar River Poetry*, she lives in Lincoln, Massachusetts, with her husband and two cats.

Back to Back

At sixteen my mother had been a swimmer.
I have seen a picture of her

poised at the edge of the pool, knees bent,
hands on knees, and smiling with her teammates.

My aunt once said back then she swam
as gracefully as Esther Williams.

But that is not how I remember her.
It is when I am sixteen and a runner

and am forever wanting to stand against her,
back to back, to see who's taller;

however much I stretch I still come up
an inch short. I've called her up

to have her drive me home from practice.
We ride home in utter silence

after my curt "thanks" and her nod,
not for lack of feeling, but for want of words.

Following her in, cleats slung over my shoulder,
I tell her to wait, I'll help her.

Already she's at the sink, peeling potatoes
and humming, one foot lifted like a flamingo.

Immigrants

To be always carrying
this stone whose own inertia
keeps doubling its weight even

as I hold it in my hand—
in truth I would cast it off
if I could
               though it cool the
sweat of my palm, suffer it-
self to be touched. Know I would

heft it at water or glass
simply to hear one thing
deafen another awake

to hear fragments falling like
stars to wound or baptize
everything
               compassed inside
the arc of its wake—but for
one thing: my grandmother gave

this stone to my mother, and
she to me, saying each hand
need have something hard to fill

its grasping, something only
time and touch can transmute in-
to an object,
                        beautiful,
this stone from Okinawa
where the grains of sand are stars.

Stitches

What can I say? I've even forgotten how
to busy my hands with scraps of needle-
work, dumb hands unwilling to commit to
what the heart won't. Instead, I sit idle
staring out windows. Nothing fits the contours
of the landscape I was born to—absence
of mountains, dense green, and salt air that smothers
like family, like the waters I breathed penned
in my mother's womb. Hard to say when I
chose this: nothing the hand does
can stitch time back to that place where mind and eye
might mend the world to wholeness. Always
two worlds. What pattern governs this surface
inscrutable as the ocean, my mother's face?

Taproot

Stooping to pull up a weed,
I think of my father
who made of weeding an art.

After work, he'd take a bucket
and his weeder from the toolshed
and clear an area of a yard he knew

would never look manicured,
whose quality would, at best,
be like something homemade.

He'd set the bucket upside down
and sit on it. Plotting a route
he'd shift the bucket, a move

so deft you might think he was just
leaning out to extend his reach.
He knew exactly where and what angle

to drive the weeder down,
north and south of the weed,
without severing its taproot.

When my father worked like this,
making small mounds he'd later
gather up in his bucket,

the dog would sniff at his bare feet
then lie down in the shade his body made.
Grounded there, he was most himself,

his hunger for perfection and control
giving way, finally, to the work itself.
It was easy to love him then.

THOMAS SAYERS ELLIS

Robert Raczka

THOMAS SAYERS ELLIS was born and raised in Washington, D.C., earned his MFA from Brown University in 1995, and currently teaches at Case Western Reserve University and in the Bennington Writing Seminars. His work has appeared in *Agni, Callaloo, Harvard Review, Ploughshares, Grand Street, The Best American Poetry 1997* (Scribner, 1997), and *The Garden Thrives: Twentieth-Century African-American Poetry* (HarperPerennial Library, 1996).

Practice: For Derek Walcott

A dank, dark basement entered cautiously from the rear.
    The first thing you saw were bass cabinets,
Their enormous backs an unmovable blackness guarding
The door.
    The first thing you heard was feedback and sometimes
Anthony Ross, our manager's kid brother, snare-
And pedal-less, pretending to kick.
    The floor was worried with slithering cords,
Living wires that lifted and looped like vines of verse.
    The cold brick walls were covered with noise
And, like it or not, several mouth-orange cardboard posters
—those trifling, Day-Glo ones that resembled sores
When the lights were ON, and sores
When they were OFF.
    The air was thick with Chinese take-out, reverb,
The young girls on us, and designer cologne.
    An orphaned microphone slept on a pillow at the bottom
Of the bass drum's navel-less, belly-impersonating, soul-shaped O

—its sense of responsibility made more evenly percussive by
A pair of congas repeatedly nursing their newborn bongos,
All meter and rhythm at once; neither dissing the pocket.
　　Floor tom. Two-faced cymbals. A hint of high-hat.
Sticks.
　　Our drummer sat facing all of this, caged, while our entire
Frontline (female vocalist included) worked out,
Breathing and counting and stepping
Like odd numbers.
　　Big Earl and Scarecrow stood behind guitars the same way
The marines at The Tomb of the Unknown Soldier
Stood behind rifles.
　　The timbales and rototoms side-by-side were
Like a finish line of chrome, the bridge (each
And every other groove) a horn's valved prose
Asked for, asked for, asked for.

Sticks

My father was an enormous man
Who believed kindness and lack of size
Were nothing more than sissified
Signs of weakness. Narrow-minded,

His eyes were the worst kind
Of jury—deliberate, distant, hard.
No one could outshout him
Or make bigger fists. The few

Who tried got taken for bad,
Beat down, their bodies slammed.
I wanted to be just like him:
Big man, man-of-the-house, king.

A plagiarist, hitting the things he hit,
I learned to use my hands watching him
Use his, pretending to slap mother
When he slapped mother.

He was sick. A diabetic slept
Like a silent vowel inside his well-built,
Muscular, dark body. Hard as all that
With similar weaknesses,

I discovered writing—
How words are parts of speech
With beats and breaths of their own.
Interjections like flams: wham! bam!

An heir to the rhythm
And tension beneath the beatings,
My first attempts were filled with noise,
Wild solos, violent uncontrollable blows.

The page tightened like a drum
Resisting the clockwise twisting
Of a handheld chrome key,
The noisy banging and tuning of growth.

Tambourine Tommy

More man
Than myth, more myth
Than freak, he would come out,
Between bands,

In a harness of bells
And high waters,
Held together and up
By a belt of rope.

His skin was thick
As friendship, his spotlit scalp
Clean as the repaired dome
Of the U.S. Capitol.

Rickety raw
And rickety strong,
He'd run from Barry Farms
To Mount Vernon

With bricks
Borrowed from the wall
Around St. Elizabeths Hospital
In each hand.

There was struggle
In his dance,
Like first-of-the-month
Or Election Day downtown.

His arms tried to
Free Terrance Johnson,
His trickster legs
Rayful Edmond.

But such drama
Never made him more
Than spectacle or more
Than beast.

No one thought
Of him as artist,
No one thought
Of him as activist.

His craft, the way
He beat himself
(head, shoulders, knees
And toes), proved he

Was one of us,
A soul searcher
Born and raised
In the District,

Proved he
Could reach in,
Blend, ease before entering,
Proved he

Was our phoenix,
Nobody's Stonestreet,
Part hustler, part athlete,
Tougher than all of Southeast.

JILL ALEXANDER ESSBAUM

Bob Kinney

JILL ALEXANDER ESSBAUM is the 1999 winner of the Katherine Bakeless Nason Prize in Poetry for her collection *Heaven*, forthcoming from University Press of New England. She was born in 1971 in Southeast Texas. She currently lives in Austin with her husband, Axel, and studies theology at the Seminary of the Southwest. A former Minchener Fellow at the University of Texas, Essbaum works occasionally as a bartender at the Carousel Lounge.

In the Beginning

It was October once, fragile as
all autumn falling out, and God wept only
at dark windows, so that no one ever knew.

Then one evening sitting deep in the sky,
east enough to stay shadow in the setting sun,
God carved into the palms of God
and rivers bled from that magnificent wound.
They clotted into continents, and it was *good*.

But only for a little while.
You see, the twins, they came out crooked.
The first was king of shivering, and the second,
brilliant as madness, but far too comfortable at the hip and thigh.

This was good, but not *as good*, for he was always cold,
and she, warm as flesh and bedstead-soft.

They stayed that way for many years.

Post-Communion Striptease

for L

Imagine me elsewhere and kneeling—
however do I survive among such textures
of salvation and praise, feeling

in degrees the stern glimmer of the chalice
where I am reflected in abstract,
an image of convexity and some malice

I've kept quiet on? I have lover's knees
and the mouth of an undiscovered
artist. Where do I belong among these

saved? If I tease my hands into reverence,
they might stay that way for good—alas,
we feed on grace with bitter condiments,

and this supper never satisfies. Should it?
I look ridiculous in dinner dress, clothed
in the humilities of well-stitched vestments

and sensible shoes. If the costume
of repentance is a new self, perfectly pressed,
then I am weary of my Sunday suit.

If I undo these buttons on the cassock of remorse,
you'll see I do not grieve for much I've done,
as well as I've forgotten my brassiere. And the farce

of wearing these impoverished stockings of devotion
is only bearable with garter snaps, half fastened.
What do I have underneath this robe? Confusion,

and the ghost of every fingerprint that's confessed
to my thighs, so much that aches to be revealed,
my ultimate wish—to be safe and undressed

at once and for good, to be uncovered without fear, bare
as a winter elm, a heart exposed yet loved
despite itself. Then, if I fall, having snared

my feet in the hems of my nakedness, I claim
whatever right deserves the maladroit:
to land between God blessed and God damned.

When the Kingdom Comes

Your mother is not your mother,
she is something else, a bird nesting in the heart
of a hollowed out tree, a saint whose skin is cool
and soft as apple-flesh, the will of God.

And your brothers are not your brothers,
they are the ash that is all of us,
scattered in its periphery,
unfortunate multitude.

Your sister, your lover, your friend
none of these are yours.
The stone belongs only to the river
which bled it smooth.

What you call your face, that canvas of mercy
which smiles with grief at even November's
drizzle and chill, is the face of someone else,
someone to come, *good tidings*,

the Christ child in a stable,
cooing as Mary tends such tiny hands.
It is her face that seems so familiar,
the answer to everything whetting the tip of your tongue.

The hairs on your head, they belong only
to themselves, and when they are done

with such a manner of belonging,
they offer themselves to stars

which outnumber them galacticly.
Everything you think is yours is not.
A father had two sons, and one of them
was heavy with desire. Friend—what's lost is found,

forever. You will wear the very best robe.
You will wear rings on every finger
of each hand. And they are not your hands.
They are God's hands,

and She formed you with them Herself
turning tricks with clay until finally
the sand sang *alleluia*, and it was good.
These hands, She will hold like treasure

all the way to Paradise, where under the glimmer of the moon
and the spark of light that fuels every prayer,
She keeps her family. And we will all be there.
And we will all *be* .

Paradise

This bridge of moon on bended knee above us
keening twilight and the snake that is
your tongue has taught itself to sing, to sing.

My hand so heavy with your hand, your eyes
brimmed curve to crease with grief, and you chant
Bread will be the body of a king,

someday. With a voice like every nectarine,
so lovely and so bruised, how I am tempted
to you, famished as a rite of spring

mid-winter underneath the tricky snow,
broom-cold, tripping fig over foot, husky
and nervous as the glassy oxen, staggering.

Remember, I am but a rib. I curve
into your spine and wrap about your heat,
fleshless as marrow, your vitreous darling.

ROGER FANNING

Kathy Wright

ROGER FANNING's first book of poems, *The Island Itself* (Penguin, 1992), was a National Poetry Series selection. He teaches in the MFA Program for Writers at Warren Wilson College and lives in Seattle with his wife and son.

The Space Needle

The Space Needle works like a pushpin,
just bigger, to put Seattle on the map.

On a field trip we all hucked loogies
from its observation deck. We learned
the Needle—complete with restaurant—went up
in 1962, a promise to President Kennedy

we would beat those Rooskies to the moon.
Okay. Good work, Apollo guys, but let's not

forget the restaurant. It's something else.
The whole place was made to rotate,
so the view keeps changing. Cool.
It prophesied a future of ease,

inertia, channelsurfing, the hollow truth
proclaimed on mall directories: YOU ARE HERE.

Baudelaire's Ablutions

Baudelaire, dead broke, nonetheless allowed himself
two hours for his morning ablutions
(warm water can be a narcotic too).
His razor scraping whiskers cleaning off
sounded like a file rassrasping
against prison bars. Never did this man
gulp a cup of coffee, bolt out the door
with a blob of shaving cream on one ear,
and go to a job. He composed himself.
Dead broke, he explored (in prose) six waterdrops
that quake in a corner of Delacroix's painting
Dante and Virgil! Meanwhile, through his window
intruded softly the spiel of a fishmonger
as well as the stench. Many, many vendors still
singsong their wares, as a sort of wishwash drizzle
inducing human animals to mope, to yawn.
We all get bored: between mainstream culture (buy things)
and nature (in this case, rain), people tend to snooze.
Poetry jolts awake the lucky few. I praise
the mirror-gazing mighty poet Baudelaire,
my hero, a fop full of compulsions,
a perfectionist to whom a single
tweezered nosehair brought tears of joy.

Oink as Taunt

In a diary found beside a skeleton
on a desert island, page after page devoted
to drooling over the elusive pigs
that thrived in the jungle. The dwindling
castaway could not kill a single one.
His crooked makeshift spears flew to countless
near misses; once a bloodspot on the path
tantalized him (his insomnia made worse
by the gruntfest of his targets foraging

after dark outside his driftwood leant-to).
Not that he starved; shellfish and fruit
were plentiful. More likely, dehydration
or a tropical fever finished him. *Then*
the monsoons brought their bounty to his leathered mouth.
But what's more poignant to me is how the pigs
came to represent a kind of heaven
to him, everything he could not have.
He longed to feast on their familial ease.
All he really needed was a little rain.
I picture him sweating when, in the last
entry, he described the glitter
of individual black hairs on a pig's back
as it fled. How can a delusion balloon
as perceptions grow keen? On page 62 he cataloged
a blue caterpillar, and even glued with spit
a bit of its blue fur to the text.
What a guy. I feel tender toward him
for leaving us a klutz's cry for justice—
albeit oblique (like some catywampus small
clay donkey from a tribe that was conquered
by the Aztecs and then by the Spaniards),
utterly useless except as counterpoint
to the oink oink success story, which continues.

Parable of the Boy and the Polar Bear

The kindly people of Vancouver, B.C.
have voted to close the Stanley Park Zoo.
Koala bears will be coaxed out of trees.
Penguins will toddle, fidgeting, into a truck.

In fact the one exotic not leaving town
is Tuck, a polar bear too frail to transport.
He's 34—same age as me—his life
expectancy in the wild. His heart couldn't take
the stress of relocating, a team of biologists

has stated. Also, no other zoo wants him. So
the toucan cries and gibbon hoots he's always heard,
the distant elephant's bassoon, will fade, then cease.
The loudest sounds will be the scuff of his pads
on the concrete pit, the click of his claws.

No doubt the zookeeps will seek other work,
and a college student will be hired
to heave-ho hunks of meat over the fence
and whistle for Tuck. And you know the day will come
when Tuck won't schlep out of his cave.
Hibernating? Not this time. How long
before something has to be done? Will the cops
go in with concussion bombs, just in case?
No sir. College boy will be issued a rifle,
or perhaps a bazooka. Listen, there are
all kinds of shit jobs in the world.

But the two basic categories are these:
the scared kid at the mouth of the cave—
he wants to do what's expected of him—
and the animal in misery
waits to explode.

JULIE FAY

Henry Stindt

JULIE FAY teaches writing and literature at East Carolina University, splitting her time between Blount's Creek, North Carolina, and Montpeyroux, France. *The Woman Behind You* was published in 1998 by the University of Pittsburgh Press. Her work has appeared in many magazines, including *The Kenyon Review, Gettysburg Review, Ploughshares,* and *13th Moon*.

Flowers

for D. W.

This is a love poem to our family,
such as it is. For our dog and
the colorful laundry heaped
in the closet, the seeds
I planted last week to line
the front walk. These
are what I'll come home to.
If all goes as planned,
larkspurs and foxgloves
opening little bird mouths
like an Impressionist's garden.

Last night you brought me flowers
that bled into themselves.
Dyed carnations.
You said you thought
they grew that way.
They don't.
They put the tips in colors.
I put them in a jar
and went to bed.

I read where someone said
Renoir's women were decomposing
flesh, green and purple
patches. I wasn't so vivid, but all night
felt a dissolution
or a healing. Several
times I woke, dreams
just out of memory's reach.

Last week, hairpins
in my mouth, I glimpsed
in the mirror full hips and breasts
working for someone else.

My body on its own
while I, an onlooker,
knew it had everything
and nothing to do with me.

"My women," R. said, "become so real, they seem
to give me orders. 'Bring me a glass of water,'
they say, or 'Let's go out into the garden.'"

Someone's missing from our family.
We chose names on Tuesday and
I changed my mind on Wednesday.
I don't know why. For now,
we'll call it fear. Today,
I have some flowers who
don't know their own color.

So here is how
the season ends:
one day I wake,
my gorgeous perennials all out
and in their mouths the doubt
and seeds shooting
out of their centers like stars.

Santorini Daughter

for Ann Elliott

Mother, blood irises unfold
beneath the window. I sit
all night, movement undetectable.
You climb through a window to a past
where you're healthy again, gathering
sheets so they settle
like limp white birds
in the straw hamper.
You scrub them at the village
basin, your voice purling
with the others', then hang
the sheets like sails
that slash the blue ocean.

It's morning and you're
awake and dying in the room
where you gave birth to me;
outside, our cobbled streets
surge downhill to sea.
I must ask you questions,
not to continue the stifled
red voices of our women.
If at any time you're in pain
please tell me. To explain

your life, you climb off the bed and
pull back the gauze curtain,
your arm curved and voluptuous
to me for the first time.
Out the window the white walls
bend down to the Aegean.
My first memory is of these
contrasts: blue and white,
men at checkers, women at water.
Old women glide in black shawls
through the windows, the white rooms
heads slightly tilted
as though just about to ask
questions. One looks birdlike
and delicate. The others
carry locks of hair reminding
us what ugly children we were.
How they hoped to turn us
into wonders, exotic butterflies!

At times I wonder how there's
life in a place where there are
only white houses round as shoulders
cutting into the sky and ocean,
everything's so still. Below the window
they're already keening. A woman
I don't recognize is just coming
around the corner, her arm curved
over a rough basket. She reminds
me of you. Oh, if only I could see
what's inside her basket.

The Mother of Andromeda

It's been years since we left Ethiopia
and I can still smell the seaweed ripe and hot
in the rocks near Joppa where she was chained.

At first, she complained, which made her no less
beautiful: that liquid hair I'd want
to get my tongue around it seemed so sweet,

the flesh that made me melt with pride. Those eyes,
they were the very meaning of life.
How we'd whisper in the old days, heads

at dawn like two conspirators' touching
on silk pillows until we had to rise,
keep others' company. She grew, as all girls do,

and grew away from me, but came back, always
with her questions. And then those tattletale
Nereids had to wreck it all. My name

alone runs red as berry juice, the tea
we'd brew and sweeten to get cool. Cassia,
cassia-juice, Cassiopeia. My daughter,

chains hissing at her wrists like alarms
to passing Perseus: was it love at first sight
or common courtesy when he saw

the serpent slither greenly and far too
sexy for his own damn good near my naked girl?
Whatever. He pulled Medusa's charmed

and severed head from his bag of traveling tricks
and that was that. The rest, they say, is history.
The headlines read: *man with flying sandals*

turns attacker back. Gets the girl.
He's not the son-in-law I would have chosen.
And she, still with grit between her teeth and toes.

Last night, from here, I saw you down below
look up at us and wonder who we were:
the monster, my daughter, my loyal husband, and the rest
turning through infinity above your sleeping heads.

Stereograph: 1903

She means two things
and leans on the gentleman's
right arm. All these years.
These two decided
to take a walk

or a boat ride. After a while
they sat down, discussed
the weather. And the tide
changed. Now they sit
above the title,
"Waiting for the Tide."

When I was nine, I waited for the girl
who looked just like me,
talked and did everything the same
at the same time. Our meeting
would take place at Compo Beach
both of us wearing our green plaid suit.

We'd sit down and face the water,
explanations unnecessary. Then
both rise and walk
into the other's territory.
Her mother was perfect—
the one who runs to me,
great concern on her face,
holding in her arms,
all the years
I've imagined her.

She gives me the gift
of this antique viewing card,
one side's almost-identical
twin pasted next to it
for someone's drawing room pleasure.

Suddenly the two women rise, walk
into the background, the woods,
arms around each other's waist.

NICK FLYNN

Elke Rosthal

NICK FLYNN will have his first collection of poems, *Some Ether*, published by Graywolf Press in 2000. In 1999 he was a "Discovery"/*The Nation* winner and the recipient of the PEN/Joyce Osterweil Award for Poetry. Flynn lives in Brooklyn and works in the New York City public schools for The Writing Project of Columbia.

Cartoon Physics, part 1

Children under, say, *ten,* shouldn't know
that the universe is ever-expanding,
inexorably pushing into the vacuum, galaxies

swallowed by galaxies, whole

solar systems collapsing, all of it
acted out in silence. At ten we are still learning

the rules of cartoon animation,

that if a man draws a door on a rock
only he can pass through it.
Anyone else who tries

will crash into the rock. Ten year olds
should stick with burning houses, car wrecks,
ships going down—earthbound, tangible

disasters, arenas

where they can be heros. You can run
back into a burning house, sinking ships

have lifeboats, the trucks will come
with their ladders, if you jump

you will be saved. A child

places her hand on the roof of a schoolbus,
& drives across a city of sand. She knows

the exact spot where it will skid, at which point
the bridge will give, who will swim to safety
& who will be pulled under by sharks. She will learn

that if a man runs off the edge of a cliff
he will not fall

until he notices his mistake.

Cartoon Physics, part 2

Years ago, alone in her room, my mother cut
        a hole in the air

& vanished into it. The report
        was deafening, followed immediately by an over-

whelming silence, a ringing
        in the ears. Today I take a piece of chalk

& sketch a door in a wall. By the rules
  of cartoon physics only I

can open this door. I want her
  to come with me, like in a dream of being dead,

the mansion filled with cots,
  one for everyone I've ever known. This desire

can be a cage, a dream that spills
  into waking, until I wander this city

planning a rose-strewn funeral. Once
  upon a time, *let's say,* my mother stepped

inside herself & no one
  could follow. More than once

I traded on this, until it transmuted into a story,
  the transubstantiation of desire,

I'd recite it as if I'd never told anyone before,
  & it felt that way,

because I'd try not to cry yet I always
  would, & the listener

would always hold me. Upstairs the water
  channels off you, back

into the earth, or to the river, through pipes
  hidden deep in these walls. I told you the story

of first learning to write my own name,
  I scrawled it in chalk across our garage door,

so that when my mother pulled it down
  I'd appear, like a movie.

Emptying Town

after Provincetown

Each fall this town empties, leaving me
drained, standing on the dock, waving
bye bye, the white handkerchief
stuck in my throat. You know the way Jesus

rips open his shirt
to show us his heart, all flaming & thorny,
the way he points to it. I'm afraid
the way I miss you

will be this obvious. I have

a friend who everyone warns me
is dangerous, he hides
bloody images of Jesus around my house

for me to find when I come home—Jesus
behind the cupboard door, Jesus tucked

into the mirror. He wants to save me
but we disagree from what. My version of Hell
is someone ripping open his
shirt & saying,

look what I did for you.

Bag of Mice

for my mother

I dreamt your suicide note
was scrawled in pencil on a brown paperbag,
& in the bag were six baby mice. The bag was
open to the darkness &
smoldering
from the top down. The mice,
huddled at the bottom, scurried the bag
across a shorn field. I stood over it
& as the burning reached each carbon letter
of what you'd written
your voice was released into the night
like a song, & the mice
grew wilder.

CHRIS FORHAN

Rebecca Freeman

CHRIS FORHAN is the author of *Forgive Us Our Happiness* (University Press of New England/Middlebury College, 1999), which won the 1998 Bakeless Prize for Poetry. He earned an MA in English from the University of New Hampshire and currently lives in Seattle, the city of his birth.

The Taste of Wild Cherry

for Kevin and Dana

The weight of the moment: immeasurable, the weight
of the self, of Dad's glance backward at us kids
shrieking and grappling in mid-winter's backseat.

At issue: a last stick of gum. At issue:
the misperception of a gesture's intent—
the insinuating jerk of someone's shoulder

sideways, the curl of an upper lip, my sour
sister's scowl, my brother's love
of torture games, my own forebearance

in the face of unrelieved suffering. I'm writing
the scene as it happens, seeking
from light and shadow the permanence of stone,

permanence of the snapped-shut ashtray that traps
smoke from Dad's smoldering cigarette. We're traveling
somewhere, the day has a name and weather, traffic

surrounds us, each car with its purpose, but I'm
intent on my sister's hair, getting a good grip,
eyeing her fist that filched the gum, my free arm

shielding my head from my brother's blows. I note
his wolfish laughter, an ache piercing my ribs,
my sister's willed, mechanical tears, my own

quiet call to God for justice. Dad's
pulled the car off the road. Faceless,
he turns, snarling words I won't recall.

My mind's on the gum he demands and slips
in his pocket, wild cherry, my mind's
on the flavor it should have had in my mouth.

I'm forging my note to the future, recording
all I know of this moment before
the moment completes itself: pearls of rain

on the windows, scent of wet carpet, song
on the radio fading—I'm saving
this one thing, nothing, smoke in my hands.

Without Presumptions

The cineplex is showing a monster movie: our autobiography.
At century's end, such blunt articulation of our condition
is useful, seeing as how we're half human

and how the tale of our being exiled angels is no longer credible
though our wings, still rooted to our backs, flap loosely
and our hearts slap sadly inside our chests.

Our heads seem suddenly oddly shaped. What crown can fit us?
Our hands are the hands of apes. We sprout coarse hair
and idle sexual fears. Lately the sky is painted

a different blue. Our stately, creaking hymns
can't bear this news. We sit and sing, roped
to the past in the midst of the perishing

present, dressed in our ancestors' threadbare clothes,
wearing their moustaches quaintly, like smudges of charcoal.
Our dumpsters overflow and smell of the day before yesterday.

Our antique gas pump and hub cap collection rusts. As the dog
adjusts to its compact, practical brain, sniffing
and shitting, we're having to find a way to live again

without presumptions—shutting the maintenance manual,
watching awhile in darkness through the picture window
pines calm beneath snowfall, old branches gathering the temporary weight.

Big Jigsaw

I've hunched so long above this puzzle
laid out on my gouged and ink-stained workbench,
I think, at last, it's unsolvable,
that the only meaning it holds is told
in the moments I feel on the verge
of understanding, and it turns me back.

The pieces: so small, so many. How they
belong together is beyond me,
though early on my mind inclined
toward an idyllic scene: a yellow field,
all jonquils, a sea, the wide horizon . . .

The dog's dish is empty. My wife and children
sleep. The house is hushed, except
for the stout hall clock that ticks its minutes.
Here in my patch of lamplight, time
dawdles, waiting for me to catch up,
though a few small hairs on my wrist
have gone white, and evening's blank encircles me.

Who made this puzzle? If I sought him out
would he hear my plea and reveal its logic?
But the hour is late, my vision strained.
How could I look for him now, though he were
waiting for me, and knew me by name?

DAVID GEWANTER

DAVID GEWANTER's first volume of poems, *In the Belly* (University of Chicago Press, 1997), won the John C. Zacharis First Book Award from *Ploughshares*. A co-editor of *The Collected Poems of Robert Lowell* (forthcoming, Farrar, Straus, Giroux), he teaches at Georgetown University and was the 1999 Witter-Bynner Fellow at the U.S. Library of Congress.

One-Page Novel

Kind, almost courtly, a   "good listener," he kept lovers
away, fearing and feeling   that long contact would reveal

some horrid prospect of his   interior—and though his soul
had stilled like seawater   left in a tank, he kept his dread

as a keepsake, caring more   for it than for the woman
who pressed herself against   his arm at work, breathing . . .

so that finally, when he met   a dark-eyed misanthrope, whose
severe answers to men masked   her own fear of exposure, of

letting her nature mix with   theirs, he thought she discovered
his hidden self, like a gleaner   in a field of glass gems

who, knowing the small   profit in some glittering cast-off,
still pockets if for another   day: what a *frisson*, he told

himself, to be seen at last,   seen through, to be found wanting
and still wanted. He took   her sourness for sympathy, criticism

for care. And she   sensing that withheld affection somehow
contented him, knew   he'd never press her to the wall:

whether a man thinks   too much of himself, or too little,
the woman is left alone.   How well their love was paid

for what it gave away,   a damp valley now blackening
beyond the smudge-lamps   of their terrace. Flanked

on the love seat,   they hug a family of strategems
while the lost coin   of the sun rolls over

the stronghold of houses,   over the reckless sea,
then gilds other houses   then rolls away . . .

Je reste roi de mes douleurs,   I remain king of my sorrows.

Divorce and Mr. Circe

When, my quiet scientific friend,
    fattening your rabbits for the blood-tap,

        the smirking pig trotting toward its noose,
did you first think of grafting a new life

to your life? Because the body is hostile
    (you once explained) it must be tricked

        into welcoming the foreign substance
that can save it, the trickle of pig

you now slip inside a man's skull. Call it
    immuno-suppression. Or call it

a violation of self, when the spores
leech through the soft Parkinsonian

ganglia, so the spastic man
    tied twenty years to a chair by

        his frantic wife, can now smack
a nine-iron and snort *Watch her go* . . . .

To graft new life is to cut one away,
    to grow from withering—

        Whatever it is you put in a brain
has first come from yours:

What remains there today
    when dog will mew, and cat

        will have his day, when a man
quivering after years of

deliberation rises from his chair at last,
    closes with steady hand the door

        his wife holds
and walks away from the house?

Xenia: Stranger/Guest

                their own flesh and blood
                and tinctures natural
                        —Herrick

I count your quick life by the minute, day, and year,
    or by the tremble your head-pit makes
beneath our shrinking family tree, where no son
        meets his grandfather
and fungus soaks the heartwood to molasses—
    One night   you plucked

the forewaters and made your mother groan, crawling
    backward from bed under a Hercules
of pain, will, nails in my arm as you hiccupped
      a first prank, knotting
your purple tie neatly round your throat,
    Joy's curtain   of flesh

parting on the near-suicide: we held your
    pink prune face, held you like a torah packed
with nitro. Cuckoo-boy, you muscled others
      from the clotting test tube
till only your heart-light flashed the screen. . . .
    Could I be   all father

and fill the line, not wince when you call everyone
    Dada, stumbling after strangers . . . as I once
stalked across the green linoleum, a baby
      Frankenstein reaching for hands
that pulled back to make me lurch further,
    Anger   Absurdity

my Janus-parents, the house of *in loco*—
    That first memory rinses the cobweb
cloth to a spectral mask, meaning
      rewoven in the day's shuttling luck
—until any moment means anything.
    The Book   of Home

reads *Praise* one day and *Blame* the next:
    we write yours with "no" and "don't" and "wait"
yet you'll become its hero. Maybe some stranger
      clouded in the woods will touch you—
a love beyond ours—and so, disguised by love
    you'll cleave your way   to your wife.

—That was Odysseus, flanked by father and son,
    chopping down men. Your son may not meet me
(we tear our books) but show him this mottled tree.
      Wands of the tree-men have jizzed the roots,
it should grow on the day of my death.
    So (I pray)   should you.

MAURICE KILWEIN GUEVARA

Janet Jennerjohn

MAURICE KILWEIN GUEVARA was born in rural Colombia and raised in Pittsburgh, Pa. His books include *Postmortem* (University of Georgia Press, 1994) and *Poems of the River Spirit* (University of Pittsburgh Press, 1996). A dynamic performer of his own work, he is Professor of English at Indiana University of Pennsylvania.

Reader of This Page

I had a dream in my mother's womb three days before I was born.

I remember I was called Andrés Cuevas and I had a different mother whose eyes were lizardgreen and who lit candles and spoke softly of how cool the breeze would be in the new year. I had many fathers in the dream; each came into my world alone with long black hair, a harelip, and twelve fingers like me. Each taught me something of wood: One walked along the coast and pointed out to me the different groves of trees; one showed me how to shape branches with fire; one had precise knowledge of metals and whetstones, while another made tiny crosses with twigs and tied them in my hair. Time passed in the dream, and one by one my fathers died of lung soreness or jaundice or of staring at the face of God in the ocean. I built each his coffin and let him sail deep in the white hot sand. Then comes the part where I am burned alive on the second day of February, 1614.

I remember you, reader of this page, as I remember the soldiers in the dream leading us through the streets to the plaza of Cartagena de Indias—the carpenter, the sorcerer, the Portuguese, the Devil's gentleman, and the peddler. Screams, chants, official proclamations, music from a shawm: The Governor held high the banner of Santo Domingo and the wooden cross I made for you, a priest I have loved my whole life, who read the final sentence, sweating.

The Hands of the Old Métis

for my father-in-law, Don Jennerjohn

One hand's arthritic and chained to the pendulum
of a grandfather clock.
It shakes a glass of orange juice to the trembling lips
when his blood sugar falls down the stairs.
Or it takes these eight pills without water
and squeezes two puffs from the new inhaler.
The other
the free hand with purple bruises and dirty fingernails
strums a blond guitar in the dark front room
or sharpens his pocket knife to the drum of thunder
or cradles two brown ferrets and a white one.
This hand works in the basement making a small log cabin
out of wood and tools and nails and glue.
It places bottlecaps of water and mealworms
at the bottom of the empty aquarium
where the orphaned bats nest.
It turns the attic globe to Canada out of boredom
or pours another cup of coffee
or weaves through the perfect ringlets of his new grandson.
The free hand of the retired electrical worker
rests solid as stone on the black remote
and falls asleep
in the brown and orange light of the Texas rodeo
at 2:00 am
his breathing machine steady as city buses through the rain.

After the Colombian Earthquake

In Pereira and Armenia rescue workers use listening devices
over mounds of cement and twisted steel. Useless.
The dead are deep in thought, putting their affairs
in order, remembering a kiss or the yellow-orange
fur-soft taste of mango. Maybe a thousand owls at midnight
can hear the girl still singing in her head. Or the mute

curse of the young man, God's heel crushing his spine.
Now even the owls have turned away
from the periodic hiss of all those little fires.
Only the ants and irridescent beetles
have the courage to march into the underworld
like flute-makers and farmers
going down the green mountain.

After the Flood

in memory of Bill Matthews

The whole valley has been under for centuries. Only the deacon
and the prothonotary had the presence of mind to die.
The rest muddle through the best we can, Melinda and I
making love in a bed that shifts in the silt
with every thrust, the yellow dump trucks
plowing water into banks of water, the letter carrier
being carried away by a current to Cincinnati,
clutching the leather pouch overflowing with poems
past the window where I kiss Melinda on the ceiling.

Now the phone is ringing and me diving naked down the stairs
to answer it. It's the other world. They ask how we are.
I say: Everything isn't paradise. The lady who reads meters
is bloating up like a balloon. The firemen are idle,
the bars stay open all night. I don't know why or who
nailed the teenager to the turning arms of the windmill. Still,
when afternoon fills the arched gallery with emerald light,
Melinda folding fresh linen in the basement,
I make her happy by cooking, oh fish in lemon and wine.

JAMES HARMS

Paige Muendel

JAMES HARMS was born in Pasadena, Calif. in 1960.
He has published two books with Carnegie Mellon
University Press, *The Joy Addict* (1998) and *Modern
Ocean* (1992). He directs the creative writing
program at West Virginia University and lives in
Morgantown, West Virginia, with his wife and two
children.

Sky

Last night a few years ago my sister
waited by the phone with a wooden spoon
and when it finally rang she beat it
and began to cry. Neither I nor
my mother made attempts to get near
that phone. Our house those years
was a block away from Christmas Tree Lane,
a row of deodars that ran without break
from Woodbury Street to Altadena Drive.
Indigenous to Nepal, the deodar is fine
in the thin air of the Himalayas, less adept
at discerning CO_2 from the solitary
molecule of smog. So now there are
gaps in the lane where the dying
trees have been cut up and dragged away.
The lights at Christmas are more obvious
and somehow garish, shocking, hanging free
where once were branches. When I was twenty

I considered lying down in front
of the crane used to remove my parents'
enormous eucalyptus. It robbed the garden
of water, they said, it would kill them
one day, drop a limb through the roof.
Instead of protest, I took a lawn chair
and a six-pack on the patio and watched the men
work their way down from the delicate
top branches, chopping for hours, finally
sawing off the trunk at the ground.
In a few years my sister's baby
will be old enough to listen attentively.
I'll walk with her through the backyard
beyond the terrace, her hand up high
in mine like a child at the fair attached
to a balloon. We'll step onto the stump,
flush now to the earth and ringed
with St. Augustine. There will be room
enough to dance with one so small.
And when she asks how tall it was,
the bluegum eucalyptus that held and hid
the stars I looked for from my
bedroom window, and caught the few that fell,
it will be easy enough just to point
to a particular spot in the sky.

As Always

　　Now that we're okay, I guess we should finish
the dishes, straighten up, attend to things so long
neglected. Just look at the plants falling from
their pots, the cat so thin; I wonder where we've been.
Everything has grown a skin of dust (what is that song
you're whistling?), and the air tastes like lilacs.
But isn't it still December? We've been gone so long.

I'm not sure of this, but I remember holding
a hand that became a glass. And then the years—
those skeins of silk slipping from their folds,
the light trapped in places like blood fixed in a bruise.
It rained every day, umbrellas looming large
in the cramped doorways, the crowded vestibules; no one
knew they were passing inward to an airy dryness so severe
their clothes fell away like feathers. And for a while
we wore our organs outside our bodies.

But as always, there were those with expertise
and grace, who knew enough to help us back
into our clothes, back into the world.
I've never held a hand so long as his
who led me through alleys between buildings
to a shaft of daylight, a circle of warmth that shrank,
as I stood in it, to a spot on the sidewalk, a dime
I picked up and carried back to the world.

If we open the door and a window,
perhaps a breeze will lift away the dust,
though I feel light enough still to blow loose
of my body. Now that we're okay, there's very little
that keeps us here, which is why, perhaps, we stay.
I no longer hear the leaves as voices gathering
beneath the trees, in the gutters.
But I would recognize your heart if I saw it.

The Joy Addict

Whales fall slowly to the ocean floor
after dying, and feed the vertical nation
for years. Like Christ, who feeds us still
they say, though I don't know.
But imagine it:
fish chasing through the bones
or nibbling what's left, the whale,

when it finally touches bottom,
an empty church.
Forget all that,
it's intended to soften
the skin, like apricot seeds and mud, or boredom.
The drift of worlds in a given day
can turn a telephone to porcelain,
open graves in the sidewalk. So that
who knows why thinking about thinking
leads to new inventions of grace
that never take, never lead to, say, what to do
with Grandmother, who is determined to live
"beyond her usefulness," which is fine,
but why won't she relax and watch the sea with me?
I wish someone would intrude on all this.
People grow tired
explaining themselves to mirrors,
to clerks administering the awful perfume.
I ask a Liberace look-alike,
"Why do you dress that way?"
"What way?" he says,
and he's right.
Who taught us to bow our heads
while waiting for trains? to touch
lumber without regret and sing privately
or not at all? To invest the season
with forgiveness and coax from it
a hopeful omen? Lord knows
the hope would heal this little fear.
But who taught us to fear?
Soon branches crackle in the windy heat
like something cooking too quickly,
dogwood lathering the empty woods
and everyone looking for a commitment
of permanence, from summer, from someone else.
Two deer the color of corn disappear
into an empty field, and I wait beside the road
for them to move. I want to see them again.

Reel Around the Shadow

On South Street, above a burning trashcan, a rasta
roasts a pigeon on a stick.

The East River moves like a whisper
past voices held in hands, the shanty towns packed

with vagrants on the lam who sing around fires as if trying to forget
their previous lives, their different hymns mingling

into moans, like widows bathing in the river
or the moon dissolving, a candle flame sputtering in its wax.

"I came here to start a band," says a man on the corner,
a Johnny Cash-type gone to seed,

his guitar case open, no instrument in sight;
he tells stories instead of singing:

"I came here to broker fortunes but left mine in my other pants.
I came here instead of marrying her, so she named him after my brother.

I came here to paint in oils but I can't afford the canvas.
It's all requests," he says. "You pick the story."

When I wander my own way, as I do now,
without lifting a heavy coin from my pocket,

it's to leave the aura of one life
for the shadow surrounding another.

Two streets down, a few over, the sudden shower
from above, an insomniac hosing his pansies on a fire escape—

it's all feathers instead of lead, the weight
of moving through America from toll to toll as if

at anytime the signs will lead us to a normal life.
While under the arch at the end or beginning

of 5th Avenue, my ghost waits
with a sack of clementines for me to finish my rounds.

It's time, he says, kissing me on each cheek,
while gypsies rustle in the trees. The statues dismount

and lead their horses toward the fountain.
And everywhere in buildings, the elevators

rise toward roofs, where angels are landing,
the world prepared at last.

ALLISON JOSEPH

ALLISON JOSEPH was born in London, England, in 1967 to parents of Caribbean heritage and grew up in Toronto, Canada, and the Bronx. She has published three books of poems: *What Keeps Us Here* (Ampersand, 1992), *Soul Train* (Carnegie-Mellon, 1997), and *In Every Seam* (University of Pittsburgh Press, 1997). She lives in Carbondale, Illinois, where she teaches at Southern Illinois University.

Chalazion

Such a funny word
for such a little thing,
a blister on the edge
the eyelid pulls over the cornea,
the thin rim we never think of
until the chalazion lodges there,
big as a boulder, small as a drop.
I seem to get one every
ten years, so every ten years
a surgeon's disciplined tools
scrape away this bit of flesh,
sealing the wound with lasers,
so I can blink again without
feeling as if my eyeball's
been scratched by a fingernail.
I walk around for half a day
with gauze swaddling my bandaged
eye, medicinal drops stinging
infection away. And I remember

the lump the surgeon showed me,
pea-sized, undistinguished flesh
gone wrong, a growth to mark
the decade's flaws, let me know
how the body can go astray
in smallest, quietest ways.

Reading Room

Back before we all became "multicultural,"
when blacks were beautiful in dashikis
and righteous rage, my father sold books
in Toronto, books of pride, sorrow, anger,

an inventory that ended up
in our living room in the Bronx,
a reading room I'd sneak into
when I wasn't supposed to,

my chore and duty there to dust
the coffee tables and knicknacks—
souvenir ashtrays from Caribbean isles,
ebony elephants and pelicans,

hand carved, foreign-wrought.
Mixed in among my mother's
nursing texts, her medical dictionary
and anatomical tomes, I found

Franz Fanon's *Black Skin, White Masks*,
a book too severe for my pre-teen brain,
polysyllabic paragraphs sailing past
my short-sighted mind, Cleaver's

Soul On Ice, which I read fervently,
loving every curse, every mention of sex,
missing the revolution in his prose
in pursuit of dirty words, staring

at the cover, captivated by Eldridge's
prison-saddened face. *Up From Slavery,*
Manchild in the Promised Land,
The Crisis of the Negro Intellectual,

poems of Cesaire and Senghor—those books
filled me with legacy, history, located me
with Jesse Owens, blazing his body
past fascism as he triumphed

at Hitler's Olympics, with Jackie Robinson
through minor and major league hatreds,
with George Washington Carver as he
synthesized genius from peanuts.

Malcolm X spoke to me from the cover
of his autobiography, black and white
photo faded, but his face still sharply
turned upward, his finger up, out,

to signal the better world beyond us.
Could I join these men if I let words
dream in me, if I struggled, didn't
settle, my gaze as bold and forthright

as Frederick Douglass's, Booker T.'s?
Wiping each book clean, I kept that room's
order, my torn rag mottled, spotted,
dark with that week's dust.

Searching for *Melinda's Magic Moment*

I wonder if I could find it,
beloved book of my childhood
whose story transported me
past ordinary black girl status
to the rarefied life of Melinda,
a brown-skinned charmer who longed

to sing and dance onstage
so everyone could roar and applaud,
captivated by her dazzling talent.
I remember its coarse cover
of woven green cloth, its large type,
pages soiled by fingers of girls

who took it from the library
to read it in their rooms,
dreaming of being as pretty
as Melinda, as adored by adults.
Every teacher loved her—
her cute nose that wasn't

too broad, her lips that weren't
too full, her head of Shirley
Temple curls. But beauty
wasn't enough for Melinda,
who wanted nothing but to be
the lead in the school play,

a production of *Alice in Wonderland*
that called for a petite blond Alice
used to pinafores, bows, white stockings.
So desperate was Melinda that she
powdered her brown skin pale,
perched a wig of fat yellow curls

on her head, put on her best dress—
one her momma kept pressed
for Easter—and she auditioned
for the role, won it, loved
all the more for her sweet
singing voice, her poise

under piled-on make-up.
She was the girl everyone cheered,
the gifted child we all hoped to be
before mirrors and magazines
told us otherwise.
So if you find this book

at some swap meet or garage sale,
if you dig it out of your mom's attic
or grandmother's basement, send it to me.
I'd like to read it again, touch it, see
if it's like I remember. And then,
I'd like to burn it.

Teenage Interplanetary Vixens Run Wild on Bikini Beach

A wash of surf guitar rolls
over cheapo credits, beach music
for three gone chicks to frug to
as they descend from their
styrofoam spaceship in stellar
bikinis, gyrating their hips
as they land on the swinginest
beach in Southern California,
hairsprayed beehives intact
after lengthy space travel.
Will our gals find romance
though adrift from their planet,
the skin they reveal through
chintzy bikinis green, clammy
with make-up? Whoever said
production values could stand
in true love's way? Whoever
said talent makes a movie?
Our trusty aliens sally forth
to find the humans of their dreams,
guys who spend all day on surfboards
rigged up before cardboard backdrops,
hoping the camera records
only from their waists up,
who can't choose between
greasy pompadours and Beatle cuts,
so they end up looking
like dead raccoons have settled in
to die atop their heads.

Our heroines must lure them
with frantic dancing so frenzied
that stretches and splotches
of melted green monster make-up
are visible to any viewer.
If you can make it past
the badly dubbed dialogue,
if you can match each alien
to her name, her guy, then
you might care if this plot's
resolved, might wonder whether
our green space babes will find a way
to fix their faulty ship.
But you don't care.
All you want to see
are poorly painted women
running amok in a sand-filled
studio set, all you want to hear
are wild guitars screeching sex
to the girl who sits beside you
in the theater's dark, her breath
quick as a go-go dancer's,
her hand the hand you clutch,
palm sweaty in yours.

LAURA KASISCHKE

Patrick Adams

LAURA KASISCHKE is the author of three volumes of poems—*Wild Brides* (New York University Press, 1992), *Housekeeping in a Dream* (Carnegie Mellon University Press, 1995), and *Fire & Flower* (Alice James Books, 1998)—and two novels, *Suspicious River* (Houghton Mifflin, 1996) and *White Bird in a Blizzard* (Hyperion, 1999).

Grace

Who can tell the difference between the state
of grace and the state of inebriation? Who

can tell the difference between love-drunk
and just drunk? Once

I turned around too fast
at a party with a drink in my hand
and splashed the shoes of a man, who said,

" Don't tell me. Let me guess. Your name is Grace."

Whether it's night or day
is a matter of indifference to the sun. Who cares

what year it was, what month, whether
the couple asleep on the park bench
in one another's arms
are lovers, or drunks? They claimed

the *Hindenburg* was lighter than air.
Everything balanced—
the lift of hydrogen, the weight of the ballast, a battleship made

out of shadow, and linen,
an emptiness like elegance
over the Atlantic, which was nothing

but a shining magazine, open. Oh, *there they go,* I imagined

the other people at this party
whispered to each other
as we wandered with our cocktails to the lawn. Imagine

that dirigible passing over
at this moment. Diamond rings, false teeth, swastikas—

all the little baggage
with which people travel. Imagine it as grace: that

moment just before
the moment in which the mystery
would like to speak to us

if we would like to listen, in which

pure pleasure, its
huge kind surge, could
pick us up together, speak

to us in human terms. The music
like honey. The temple
full of monkeys. To show us how much greater

is the game than any player.
How much brighter
is the porchlight
than the chalklight inside a moth.

Air pressure.
Air temperature.
The weight of the passengers.
The lift of the oxygen.
Everything balanced.
Everything gauged. But then

the fear of water again—of flight, of public restrooms, of
open spaces, bees,
bridges, traffic, grace.
The *Hindenburg*

was landing
when it suddenly became

brighter than the sun at noon.
It had no weight.
In Lakehurst, New Jersey, all the dogs barked.
It was Ascension Day.
The month was May.
1937.
A light rain.

The *Hindenburg* was landing.

We all know *nothing*
is lighter than air,
but it sure felt that way.

The papery
disintegration, the star of a girl dropped
onto the world, the bird
tossed right along

with its cage into the flames.
In heaven, the burning skeleton.

For *years* he called me Grace.

Oven

The fruit is ruined, but the bread is baked.
The meat is no longer raw
on its tin plate

but where
is the hooded cloak
of a warm summer night, the new lover drunk
in the middle of the day, the possum with its
damp white-hearted face? Or the woman

turned to cinders
one morning at the beach. *She*

was a teenager, wearing
a bikini—
who is this? Who is this?

There are chalk
drawings on the walls
but they are crude. What
can they tell us

of what the birds really tasted
when they pierced the pale blossoms
for the first time with their tongues?

The empty church.
The empty school.
The theater, empty, the play is done.

The oven as womb.
The oven as grave.
So much no one
ever needs to say. All

this singing and saying—for centuries—the same.

While inside the oven, not a sound not a sound.
The path leads in, the ashes out.

Please

Stay in this world with me.

There go the ships.
The little buses.
The sanctity, the subway.
But let us stay.

Every world has pain.
I knew it when I brought you

to this one. It's true—
the rain is never stopped
by the children's parade. Still

I tell you, it weakens
you after a while into love.

The plastic cow, the plastic barn.
The fat yellow pencil, the smell of paste.

Oh, I knew it wasn't perfect
all along.
Its tears and gravities.
Its spaces and caves.
As I know it again today

crossing the street
your hand in mine
heads bowed in a driving rain.

JAMES KIMBRELL

Jennifer Eriksen

JAMES KIMBRELL's first book, *The Gatehouse Heaven*, was selected by Charles Wright for the 1998 Sarabande Book's Kathryn A. Morton Prize. Among his awards are a "Discovery"/*The Nation* Award, a Ruth Lilly Fellowship, and *Poetry*'s Bess Hokin Award. He teaches in the English Department at Kenyon College and is the director of the Ohio Poetry Circuit.

True Descenders

after Luca Signorella's The Damned Cast into Hell

No matter how thunderous the chorus
    of their damnation, surely the wine-veined
gold-tipped fornicators must relish
some pleasure in the last hurling spiral
    down the spines of all the bat-winged devils.

Like the star-shaped sugar maple leaves
    plummeting toward the thick asylum
of my own backyard, that warped infinity
of roots, it's impossible that their descent,
    whether here or from the constellations

over Orvieto, could ever be anything
    other than beautiful, their harshly bronzed
breasts and buttocks growing more luscious
with every imaginable sin. And what's
    to be made of Saint Michael and his flock,

drawing their cloud-glazed swords,
    torsos wrapped in steel? Especially now,
when the landscape's flustered, it's difficult
not to begrudge the high archangel
    his stock of feathers, his cosmic lock

of windblown hair, his breastplate, cool
    to the touch. It's a point the leaves
don't have to argue, whether to give in
to the pull of a soon-to-be-iced
    patch of autumnal earth, or to resist and so hang

perpetually rigid, heavy-legged traitors
    to lust. Suppose our own innocence,
in that red November dusk at the end
of the world, should remain that righteous,
    should take up its silver armor against

the quicker passions ready to tumble
    in any celestial bed, we'd see how it is
that we've always lived in the house
of at least two Gods, one of nipples and random
    erections, one of devotion to the virtuous

invisible, and that to truly worship either
    is to finally love the other. If
the swollen, cartwheeling transgressors
of desire begin to desire once more,
    who'd not let the blue-with-death demons

untie their hands and follow their
    laughing down the hall? Who could
not feel their own body going holy?
Who would not take a lover then
    and guiltlessly watch the wrist-ropes fall?

A Slow Night on Texas Street

Pusan, South Korea

After the dancing ended, and the Russians
Had boarded for Vladivostok, just then: ·
A kettle of water, a bottle of wine, a dimly
Audible scuffle of soldiers in the street,
Drunk in the middle of a cease-fire.

That was all that could be heard from the tables
And chairs, from the room with its mirrors
Vaguely aglow. No women in the corner
Selling drinks, no lonely GI mouthing
The words. A silence long enough to hold.

And then, as if it had never happened: music
Again, glasses touching, a couple hurriedly
Retaking the floor, the bartender shouting.
Counting his change, and someone writing
Someone's name in the breath-wet window.

Self-Portrait, Jackson

The trees are hopelessly overstylized, the sycamores
And breeze-pulled willows, the live oak branches'
Groundward sprawl gracing the State Street mansions.
There's the hospital where I was born, and just beyond
The Jewish Cemetery, the manicured lawns where I
Was schooled in all the classical ways of feigning
Education. Strange how a place claims you, and doesn't.
How you wheel right in from past to present inside
A rented car, as if someone were waiting, an old lover
Perhaps, anxious to greet you, to be impressed, as if
That lover were the place itself. But home holds
No magnolias behind its back. And when you step
Into the parking lot all slicked up and wrong again,
Nothing welcomes you like the glint and glare between
Clouds which fail to arrange themselves, which loll
As they always have above their noon-cast shadows.

Mt. Pisgah

It was the middle of the night and I had lived
A long time with that country, with the hay
Rakes and rock paths and the beam bridge
Above the snake-thick waters. It was
The middle of the night so far into the field
The deer began not to notice the moons
In the shallow bean row puddles. Thar's how dark
Fell over the road that led into town and kept us
All from moving. Still, when the train passed,
Milk shook in its bucket and the earth sank
In a little. So each year when the corn shrank
Back to stubble, the mud strewn with husks,
More than anything silence grew tall there
Between the kitchen window and the shed's
Roof and the one note rust made in the stuck
Weather vane, in the rooster holding north.

MARY LEADER

Richard Gess

MARY LEADER, as Assistant Attorney General of Oklahoma and as Referee to the Oklahoma Supreme Court, practiced law before coming to poetry. Her first book of poems, *Red Signature*, won the 1996 National Poetry Series and was published by Graywolf in 1997.

Portrait
"Fritz Kreisler"

[addressed to the photographer whose name is not stated on the reproduction I have in hand, although the caption does supply the year the picture was taken: 1913]

The emphasis on the dull and the glossy
    Surfaces, especially of the violin-body,
      Which has, in this light and shadow, both; &
The matte of the violinist's cheek, his jaw, his brow, below
The gleam of his up-combed waves;
The flat wool of his coat, lapels & sleeves,
    Setting off
The coin-like tie-clasp,
The medal-like watch-fob,
The strange lozenge of glass toggled on its long silk ribbon;
The emphasis on little things:
The ridge where his lower lip ends,
The violin's four pegs angled differently, catching
    Different degrees of dim and shine, near and echoing
The fabric-covered buttons of his vest: both designs for thumb & forefinger;

The small things:
The clitoris inside a woman,
The shutter-button on your camera:
The places that open and close and tune and control.
Don't ask him to smile.
Don't ask him to make less specific
        The tilt of his head.
Don't ask him to move his right knuckles
        From where they indent his waistcoat.
Don't ask him to lift the violin and the bow
        Hanging from his left hand
        And put them into playing position.
Don't ask him to avert that direct gaze of his, coldly assessing you though it is.
He would just as soon you did your job, accomplished
        This session with expertise and dispatch so
He can get on to lunch with a woman.
He does not want you to join him for lunch.
He does not want to have to come back and do this over
        So take whatever pictures you will now.
He looks on you more or less as a tailor.
He expects you to make him look good, but
He cares nothing for you, and is not curious about your work
He does not see it as comparable to his own form of virtuousity
He may—no, he will—he will notice
The crumbs in your moustache from
The cold roll you crammed into your mouth with your coffee.
He doesn't care.
He may, as small talk, describe your slovenliness to his companion at lunch.
He wants her to want him.
He will give her those intense eyes, his head cocked at
The angle he strikes
        Habitually, as now, for you, habitually subtle.
        An afternoon—or part of one—in the Hotel Blank.
He will not fuck her in his shirt—he can wait—and prefers it naked,
        And under the covers,
        With his eyes closed, so as to smell
The perfume and the cunt, so as to feel
The hair massed in his hands, so as to hear

The every noted moan, because he is working on
The Sibelius,
The Concerto in D minor, and needs to fill it full of
        Someone's longing for himself.

Madrigal

How the tenor warbles in April!
He thrushes, he nightingales, O he's a lark.
He cuts the cinquefoil air into snippets
With his love's scissors in the shape of a stork.

Hear the alto's glissando, October.
She drapes blue air on her love's shoulders,
On his velvet sleeves the color of crows.
Her cape of felt and old pearls enfolds her.

How the baritone roots out in May!
His depths reach even the silence inside
The worms moving level, the worms moving up,
The pike plunging under the noisy tide.

Hear the soprano's vibrato, November,
Water surface trembles, cold in the troughs.
She transforms blowing hedges into fences,
She transforms scarlet leaves into moths.

Impetus

A man half Alan and half Uncle Arnold
Stopped by the millinery shop to mention:
"Cursed be any God who allows the old
To flop on this regular a basis." Shun

Any omnibus which is a tourists' tour,
Any present for the apparition of a Virgin
As in the Rinuccini Triptych's flames. Our
Tongues one by one by one by one cave in.

To get to the shop he went up a perpendicular
Road; the carriages had to be strapped to it.
He heard the dots in the park say, "No end
To this lot, they're all commonplace." I

Heard him say. "Right, but you err to be seeking
Minimal falls. Pastoral falls take flight:
You, Brook, release me, lift my weak king."
Back God comes, nailing horses' hooves to light.

Skin

Uncurl the sheet of vellum and there
Are the obscurely interrupted complex roses,
The letters of English.
The vine with a thousand ears,
The decay of the tempera and the decay of the vegetative shell,
The decay of addition, of cracking, and air with its vigor,
Which grinds or is perhaps shifted away
Like the day.
Uncurl the sheets, there is in them the decay of the trembling recorder,
The decay of the dipping hands, of the chant, of the anvil in the ear,
The decay of the swallow-like bell-tolls, bolting from the tower.
Did the scrivener will with one's utter heart the snail's-pace risk?
Catch it in the bell sound? Smell it in the domicile rain?
To love the thin vellums and the erasure, scraping on them . . .
To love anything,
You must be prepared to rip, or bear its trace.

m loncar

m loncar, born in Youngstown, Ohio, received his BA from Miami University and his MFA from the University of Michigan. A filmmaker and photographer, he has lectured in the English and Film and Video departments at the University of Michigan and is currently employed at the University of Michigan Museum of Art.

as my cat eats the head of a field mouse he has caught

i can only think of him as
a kitten on my head, that strange
way my brother and i used to carry him
walking around the living room the way
egyptian women bring water into villages. is this
the root incident of his head problem/fetish? is this
the event that led him to hate heads? i remember when i
ate my first head. it was certainly not out of hatred,
more a curiosity, like what's under her
skirt, what's going on in her head as she
lifts it and I catch the echo of my body
hitting the floor.

one night america: a boy and his blowtorch

will tear through you with his tangled
fingernails and sour memories   open   filled
4 bleeding hearts in his chest   you'll throw
daughters and sons and black coffee at him
but he'll stare at each and weep and worship
their bodies are like machines to him   and he'll
be trying to love them without erections like
he wanted just to inhale them for a minute
and they'll love him all the more   because
in america   they love crucifixions   flat
squirrels and birds   those things and of course
evangelists and mass murderers and movie stars
i myself like those people plenty you know
but no one as much as tina turner who has been
known to at times take control of this steering wheel
and might i add i have been known to have enjoyed
the rides   and as for that blowtorch   he always
liked to leave the people he loved   something to
remember him by   sometimes a wired metal headboard
above their bed   or sometimes   even something small
like iron railroad tracks running through their kitchens

peoria

we were drinking coffee (of course)   when in walks
these two punk rockers   one full of body piercings
and nails in his skin   the other with a blood orange red
mohawk   smoking a pipe   the one with the nails also has
a dog collar around his neck and hands the leash to angelina
who flattered   starts leading him all around the place circling
tables   and into the bathroom then the one smoking the pipe
(it musta been about 200 degrees) comes up to me and says
listen here kid

we're worried about you
we love you and we
don't want anything to happen to you
everything will be all right
it'll be ok

kisses me

then gets up grabs the leash from angelina
leads the one with the nails in him
and they get in their van and drive off

jesus tim sometimes i have no idea
        what the hell is going on

kentucky

hello sir i'm glad you're here we
were just trying to pet the cows and
have a little fun with the electric fence boy
we didn't mean to trouble anyone least of all
the owner of such a fine looking field and my but
that is a fine looking cow you have there as well as
a fine looking pasture in this light it almost looks quite
blue they really do have blue grass here don't they that's what
i hear blue grass and not a whole set of teeth in the state

JAMES LONGENBACH

Emma Dodge Hanson

JAMES LONGENBACH is the author most recently of *Threshold* (University of Chicago Press, 1998) and *Modern Poetry After Modernism* (Oxford University Press, 1997), essays on contemporary American poets. His poems have appeared in *Nation, The New Republic,* the *Paris Review,* and *The Best American Poerty, 1995.* He teaches at the University of Rochester.

Learning Window

Morning swoops down on her with words, chews,
Regurgitates. She swallows greedily

But will not sing.
                    So much to be hungry for.
She dreams of mockingbirds, old women who speak
The minds of others as easily as their own.

She twirls her tongue, practicing the feeling—
Sibilants, vowels. Imagine breaking the shell

To floating free of silence, knowing from birth
All the sounds your parents make.
                              Look at them.
Mouths hovering above the bed each night
As if to consume the world with singing.

She dozes, waits for them to disappear. Even

A sparrow, dark, plainer than darkness, must listen
Only to the song its mother knows—
Practicing in silence a one-note vocabulary.

Window shine.
                    Pain rising in the mouth, hunger, no,
A tooth, the will to chew.
                    They're here again.
Tufted, possible, beyond the glass, envelope
Of light in which she's waiting, a throat,

For a reason to believe there's a world inside.

Undiscovered Country

1. The Return

Snow, rocks darker than any shadow in the world.
We glimpsed another life below us—cottages, goats—

But never imagined it would be so difficult.

Mountains made us long for the clouds. Trails
Gave way to roads, roads to thoroughfares—

Where were we?
                    When we came to a village
We lay down in the weeds as we were told—hungry—

But if anything the stars seemed brighter then.

We waited. Peered through stalks and umbels
Across the flat ground.
                    And when we heard them
Running towards us we buried our faces
In the mud and did not move.

                        Minutes, hours—
They combed the field. Had we been lied to?

Just when our heartbeats seemed unbearable
One of us broke free—we followed—speaking
In a language we no longer recognized—

Where am I?
               They wrapped our shivering bodies
In towels. Fed us. Tried to look in our eyes.

2. Walking Upright

Some things we missed. Snow mold. Ferrous taint
Of soil in our mouths.
                     Once, sunlight
Overhead, we found a knot hole, peered inside—

Two eyes, tinier than ours, glistening, contained.

They vanished when a cloud slipped past. Chipmunk?
Bat? We couldn't imagine it looking back

At our dark faces. But as we foraged, day
Receded like a furrow. Distance. We tipped

Up our chins, widened our outlook on heaven.

Trees—mountains furred in green—so many shades
It seemed space were grafted onto time.

Who'd thought one moment could contain such
Variation? Balance. And the possibility
Of something lost.
               Then tree tops swept
The clouds into a fury—peaked, impatient—leaving
Us behind. Sky pressed down close. No shelter.

No proportion. Nothing between our faces
And infinitude—but when we opened our eyes

We weren't alone.
                    Night. Crackling stars.
Wings ploughing the black pasture between them.

3. Remains to be Seen

We were far from shore, then close, then farther still.
Someone waited—a stroke. We couldn't see

The boat but heard it: one oar broke the surface,
Paused, then slapped again.
                              From anywhere
Stars were a blur, refracted through layers of dense fog.

Leaves floated past us. Duckweed. If we lurched

It was from boredom, the feeling of movement almost alien
Now that we'd grown so large.
                               The boat drew
Nearer. We squinted. Inspected the rusted gunnels,
Oarlocks squealing as they swiveled and turned.

Reckless? From her face, the way she dropped
The oars, reeled the line, we knew we were safe.

Gray, severe, her features, fog—everything mingled
As if the world had forsaken boundaries—

I confronted her, eye to eye, but the longer she stared
The more I sank inside myself, sunrise stark
Above the water, a weight, a lure.
                                   I was already missing
When she let me go.
                     Dawn, dusk, we circle the island
And nothing portends. Fireflies drip and twirl.
Night's face. Malingerer. Remains to be seen.

4. Lying Down

When the first one swooned it was difficult not

To follow. In fields, never the mines—eyes lifted
Skyward, craving emptiness.
                    Eyes rising
The way water, learning weight, falls down as rain.

We'd learned a dome of ether lies above us—
Weightless, sure. A dream of purity which mixed

With water generated shapes we've trusted.
                              The body.
Ground we bothered with pickaxe, adze, believing
—No evidence—there was something beneath.

But a haunting persisted.
                    There, stretched out
Breathless on the ground, a separation
Opens, lip to cloud, a rift of self from self—

Another life, the world above us
                          now within—
A memory, no moats or walls, the body withering
Into former knowledge as the fields turn brown.

Men row aimless, dazed, where once they'd toiled
Behind bullocks. Sleepless nights.

Dolphins gamboling weightless through the trees.

5. Ascension

Because there is a car there is a field bending
Like arms to keep us dry. Because there is a field

Flowers fall from the sky to cover the car, souls
Linked arm in arm along the Finchley Road.

Staves and bundles, hedges, brickstacks.
                                        For all
We know, these fields are long past harvest.
Ground pocked with footsteps, rutted by cellar holes.

As far as we see, mountains are shadow and light.

The car rolls forward. Petals coat the windshield
And arms reach out to sweep them away.
                                        Once
A lamb jumped straight into the air beside the chapel.
We saw it as children, then tried to see it again.

Cottages, farms.
                        Road dividing the field—
Car generating the road as it turns, as arms beget
Flowers, a lake in the field, and the island
Floating there, serene.
                                Gates close behind us,
Long arms of the stars collecting what we'd seen.

Because the only consolation for having been known
Is being forgotten. Because there is a car.

What You Find in the Woods

Nothing in the air to call me here—
Trees recede into the dark circumference
Of the hill and everything's reduced
To the chilled circle of its lesser self.
No muddy spoor, no red sleeve of a fox
Against snow. But things accumulate
As if from nothing. Nests of broken glass.
A frozen mess of feathers, kicked, upturns
The bird intact, the tiny beak a rictus.

Once, when I lived near woods like these,
I followed older boys who stumbled
On a child's body wrapped in wool—nothing
Left but sinew tangled with bones.
What's this? Sycamore bark that's flaked
Away like skin. Trees shift uneasily—
A hawk, wings too lofty for this wood,
Descends to look at me; its head turns once
Before the branch it rests on breaks away.

Then nothing. Silence thinning on a hill
Too low for speculation on our lives—
There's nothing here I don't already know.
So more than anything, more than the slow,
Determined beat of wings, I'm on the lookout
For the bone, the skeleton half buried
In leaves, the body sprinkled hastily
With dirt and sticks, the open hand, the face
Disheveled and no stranger than my own.

SHARA McCALLUM

SHARA McCALLUM was born in Jamaica and immigrated to the United States at the age of nine. Her first book, *The Water Between Us*, won the 1998 Agnes Lynch Starrett Prize and was published by University of Pittsburgh Press in 1999. Her poems have appeared in *Antioch Review, Iowa Review, Virginia Quarterly Review*, and elsewhere. She is a member of the MFA faculty at the University of Memphis.

Fugue

1.

angels' voices lost to air
lemons relinquishing
their scent to the breeze
in the garden if I could
hold my guitar again
be music thrumming
in my hands
all day the sun
sifts through the trees

2.

veins are black birds
clawing beneath skin
doctor says to swallow
the pinks yellows reds
but once I heard Jesus
speaking in my voice
once

3.

words are water
slipping through my hands
where is Migdalia?
when will she bring the child?:
so grey so blue her eyes
like the sky like the moon
even now
just before dark

Collage

We are a symphony of scissors,
stirring the windless air.
Cutting scenes from old magazines,
gifts from the houses Mummy cleans,
we are ballerinas and swans
and live in rooms with chandeliers
and mirrors, where everything gleams.
Perfume bottles dangle
like overripe fruit from trees.
Girls in pinafore dresses
picnic in flowerless fields.
Lions cower beneath lambs.
Bottles of Elmer's bloom

from our hands.
We paste ourselves
to the walls and paper
sticks to our fingertips,
grey and pink threads
bury themselves
beneath our skin.

In the Beginning

In the garden of dusk
the father is being born.
One part of his mind
crystallizing into salt,
clear and stinging as the sea.
One part unhinging
like the fruit of the tree
plucked too soon from its stem.
Here, he will learn to speak
in the voice of the lord
and believe that sound
to be the echo of himself.
Here, he will perfect
the loneliness that,
in its brilliance,
like the sun, blocks
all others out.
Years later, night
falls in the garden,
falls across the leaves,
across the grass, leaving
a trail of silver light.
His daughter is born.
He does not know her face.

The Deer

A body sinks and rises
when it drowns.
So the deer, dead
one week in our pond.
First the tip of the head
visible, then gone
till this morning
as your face rose
from the steaming bowl.

Through the kitchen window,
I watched you wade
to the water's edge,
shovel in hand;
your body lost to me
in that tangle of limbs:
arms, leafless trees.

CAMPBELL McGRATH

E. Lichtenstein

CAMPBELL McGRATH is the author of two chapbooks and four volumes of poetry including *Capitalism* (University Press of New England/Wesleyan, 1990) and *Road Atlas* (Ecco, 1999). The recipient of Guggenheim and MacArthur fellowships, he teaches creative writing at Florida International University and lives with his wife and sons in Miami Beach.

Capitalist Poem #36

We've got this cheese down here to give away,
tens of thousands of pounds of cheese.

We're trying to establish procedures and specifications,
rules to discourage speculation and hoarding,

guidelines to foster the proper use of this
extraordinary resource. What we need is a system.

I mean it. Not one damn piece of cheese
leaves here until we get this thing figured out.

Florida

If they'd had a spark of wit or vision
it would be known today as Cloudiana,
in honor of the mighty Alps and Andes
assembled and cast westward as rain
and thunder each and every afternoon.

If they'd understood the grave
solemnity of the sublime
it would be named for the great blue heron:

for longevity, the alligator;
for tenacity, the mosquito;
for absurdity, the landcrab.

If they had any sense
of history
it would be called Landgrab,

it would be called Exploitatiania,

for the bulldozed banyans,
lost cathedrals of mahogany and cypress,
savannahs of sawgrass and sabal palm,
mangroves toiling to anchor their buttresses,
knitting and mending the watery verge.

Beautiful and useless, flowers
bloom and die
in every season here, their colors dissemble,
soft corpses underfoot.

If there was any justice in this world
it would be named
Mangrovia.

The Florida Anasazi

From above it's a dickie or a verdant tie skewed sideways, banana or schlong, skull of a prehistoric mammal with lower mandible removed and Okeechobee for its eye, a moth-eaten pennant hemmed with blue water, a peninsular thumb bruised a dozen shades of green, emerald fronded jungle and sandy palmetto veldt and the predominant olive dun of once-cleared land reverting to scrub. And from the plane one sees, throughout Florida, titanic etchings upon the ground, quadrants of scarred earth that in their obscure figurative squib resemble the sacred patterns of a primitive mythos, the song lines of aboriginal Australians, or the vast animal figures of the Nazca plateau, or the pictoglyphs of the ancient Anasazi, sun-bleached ochre against canyon wall, fertility symbols and animal visages, banded armadillo and antler flange, mischievous coyote, flute-bowed Kokopeli, so different from the local totems, backhoe, chainsaw, roadkill, stripmall, the alligator-headed figure known to us as The Developer who works his trickery upon the people of the tribe, pilfering communal goods, claiming to produce that which he despoils. This is his signature, this marked and scarred earth, a palimpsest of greed and grand plans gone wrong, a promissory text of spectral subdivisions, roads and cul de sacs that never were, premonitory ghost cities rising like the ruins of the Anasazi in reverse, their abandoned pueblos and cliff dwellings slipped into empty rungs on the ladder of need, a civilization as inconspicuous as lichen, vanished after centuries with little to mark its tenure but rock drawings and the shards of earthenware vessels, a midden heap of piñon nuts, a loom shaft carved from juniper wood. The Florida Anasazi aren't here yet, but you can tell they're coming. The mark of their ruin has preceded them, to help them feel at home, and so that we may know them when they arrive.

Jack Gilbert

Take a hammer to the amphora of soft Euphrates clay
and it will fracture meticulously there, and there,
and there, the way a sentence yields at the invisible
seams and faults of grammar's fluid syntactic
tectonics. Take a chisel to the mountainside—basalt,
gabbro, porphyry—and, well, what did you expect?

Jeffrey Lee Pierce

Jeffrey Lee Pierce is dead, at age 37, in Salt Lake City, Utah.

R.I.P., J.L.P.

What tenuous clichés, the unrusted corpse and the early grave, stupidly traditional rock and roll icons, though he was anything but a traditionalist, and so it rang as a double surprise, coming across his obit in the *Times*—that he was gone, yes, prematurely and forlornly; and that they had deemed his passing worthy of notice, esteemed him an artist of such cultural significance, because I really hadn't known there were that many others out there listening, that many who valued his music as I did, took him seriously, saw him play half-a-dozen times across the years, the many permutations of the Gun Club behind him, early 80s blues-punks and middle era noise mongers and the elegant, raw-boned, in-exile band, but always the same old Jeffrey Lee, spaghetti epic in a Fassbinder overcoat singing "Ghost on the Highway" and "She's Like Heroin to Me" with the atonal wail of a leopard-skin banshee, a bleached-blonde voodoo-doll of Elvis circa "Flaming Star" spraying gunslinger guitar solos to the western wind, sawed-off and smacked-out, smiling at the crowd with hip condescension informed by self-awareness, or so I always felt, such was the image I had composed of him, though it may be he was just a junkie-with-an-attitude nobody much cared for, as they say in the rock and roll "press," I have no evidence to the contrary but the testimony of my ears, and I'm not suggesting he was any kind of genius, but I do think he was good at what he did.

And the more I learn about anything

the more I respect that: being good; skill, craft, a knowledge of form;

after which comes passion, commitment, belief in the ideal, faith in the power of noise to transcend the graffitied walls of this cinderblock sub-basement rock club of a world;

which is art;

which resides in the ear of the beholder.

So have I bent to the grace notes and troubling invective of his music, a dark embryo hungry for oxygen, an unfinished chrysalis of ecstatic rage. So have I hunched to listen, in the small hours, as for a benediction or sonic transcendence, keen or trill of some message expertly encrypted. Did I find it? No. But then, I didn't really expect to. Not yet. Maybe never, now that Jeffrey Lee is dead, though I am only one of many still listening, at least I have learned that much, one of many bound to bear witness to what lives on long after the voice of the singer has gone.

A song.

There. Can you hear it?

VALERIE MARTÍNEZ

VALERIE MARTÍNEZ's first book of poetry, *Absence, Luminescent* (Four Way Books, 1999), won the Larry Levis Prize and received a Greenwall Grant from the Academy of American Poets. Her poems have appeared in many journals and anthologies, including *Parnassus, Prairie Schooner, Confluence, The Bloomsbury Review, The Best American Poetry 1996* (Scribner, 1996), and *Touching the Fire: Fifteen Poets of Today's Latino Renaissance* (Doubleday, 1998). Her work is forthcoming in *American Poetry: Next Generation.* She recently has completed a volume of translations of Uruguay's Delmira Agustini. Martínez lives in New Mexico.

Camera Obscura

> For there is a boundary to looking.
> And the world that is looked at so deeply
> wants to flourish in love.
> —Rilke, "Turning-Point"

For a moment there is no periphery:
    the pupil, inky and pooling,
up against telescopic glass, fixes
    on the planet, perfectly etched,
a chalky-ash, eye launched
    upon mirrors and lenses, eye
traveling and transfixed.

I step away so others can look.
     Step away to the present hour,
bitter cold, numbness in my hands,
     one eye wandering the distant
hills, moonlit, one eye stunned
     still as a glass relic.

Is it love? Love of the world
     now collapsing to a mote,
a shrinking place in the expanding
     universe, now at this very moment,
in the crater of the heart?

I ask to look again;
     I cannot believe the crush
of distance. There it is,
     like a schoolbook drawing, Saturn,
past the eye's first boundary, brimming
     on the second, not even near
the sight of a stronger lens,
     the disheveled astronomer at four a.m.
bent over an eyepiece, looking out
     of the knowable world, and shuddering.

It is all boundaries converging.
     And looking, as I shudder,
in my breathlessness, a kind of disbelief,
     I find the love of loves.

Later, in a bed beneath all those layers
     of light-years, beneath cosmic dust,
galaxial bent light, comets, ozone,
     fir trees, smoke, cabin roof,
we revel in the nearness of what collapses
     and meets. No measurable space
between us, molecules crushed
     to the periphery of our bodies,
the planet compressed to my eye,
     swallowing breath from your mouth—

distance collapsing, distance overcome
    by science and desire,
distance O distance undercut.

Ever So, Between

1.

Here they stand, rotund, and undiluted by grief.
Their hands are full of violets, invisible.
The velvet of their garments blows
almost imperceptibly over the ground.
Heaven is a room hemmed in by wishes
recently neglected, near enough to perfume
          the skin

      here, in the second realm
      where paradise lingers,
    something on the tongue
      we vaguely know.
    The garden doing its best
      to reach through
   lilac, cherry blossom, cool
    breeze ruining the heat.
  Wishes slip even as we clutch
  and clutch. Even as we grin.

2.

We cannot explain our love of the mountains,
clay-red, dotted with piñon, chamisa, yucca.
Because it may be the expanse between them,
the sky which fills the space, immense,
the breath opened up like a holy book
blank and ever-blue, on and on.

3.

Now the gangs appropriate
the Virgin of Guadalupe.

Needled into their arms.
Screened onto cotton.
Scribbled with boxy, tilted
gang tags for protection.

The pallbearers wear her image
over and over until it blurs
under the casket, the boy
with a bullet in his neck.

They feel him passing over.
They choose her because pain
is the passing, reaching through.

They know it.
They know it and know it.

4.

The girl feels her body as nothingness.
Nothingness makes her an angel.
Angels may not be unloved.
Unloved, the body hides itself,
itself—or disappears into air.

5.

They surround themselves with creatures hopefully injured—
a puppy with four broken legs, crushed by a yellow car.
They fill the tub and work its tiny limbs, numb. It's forgotten
they should move, lies with a stick all day, tail wagging.
Lively half-life.

Who could? Why? Animals because they come and go?
Creatures of another world and ours?

6.

under the surface
the sea
echo & blur of voices
every physical thing
                 undulating
slowed-down time
blue-green
distant kin
they   sing

on the surface
frightened
dark & invisible
the behemoth   beneath
impending
enormousness

7.

The place on the mesa.
The heat and no sleep for two days.
The corn pollen.
The medicine man chanting over her.
The smoke of the pipe in her lungs.
The talisman, feathers, terrible hunger.
The liquid drunk.
It makes her vomit

into the buzzing lack of heat and the eyes
opening to a silhouette graceful
as the antelope who speaks so clearly
every syllable is the umbilical thread tugging
ever so gracefully between
the overlapping, world into world.

8.

It is why the creeping down
is like the knees, the crossed
legs, forehead to the ground,
the hands pressed together
and words a delirious fever
could be all or one anguish,
devotion, bereft love, deliverance.

9.

I step into the garden (and its hint
of bodies) where the roots spin
into trunks and branches, into
yellow blossoms then fruit.
Elemental as even the house
upon the ground, hemmed in
by air.

The layering. The interpenetration.

I say *hint of bodies*. I say *ocean
once over this*. I say *every creature
before us*. I say *this world
and the others* reaching
through, reaching
through.

KHALED MATTAWA

KHALED MATTAWA was born in Benghazi, Libya, in 1964. He is the author of *Ismailia Eclipse* (Sheep Meadow Press, 1995) and the translator of two books of Arabic poetry. His awards include a Guggenheim Fellowship, an NEA translation grant, and an Alfred Hodder Fellowship from Princeton University. He lives in Durham, North Carolina, where he is finishing a doctoral degree at Duke University.

Cricket Mountain

The bridge under our wheels moaned, some said, because it was built in a time of war. Others were more specific—it moaned because of the two men buried in the concrete. Rommel built, the British maintained the asphalt after he was driven away. My father drives across it with the car lights off. The haze from the city is enough to show the way, he explains. Then we stop by a channel that carried sea water to the salt fields. There are no birds, not even the sudden flop of a fish, or the rumble of the city's thousand pariahs that roam the streets and howl through the night. The sound of the crickets crawls like a creature wanting itself to be known, yet quick to withdraw. My father rests his hand on my shoulder to quiet me. Then soon there is nothing in the world but crickets' hum, an ordered machinery, a vibrating zone, the sound wrapping you like a shroud. If you close your eyes you can almost see the mass of their history, the infinity of their births and deaths, the design of their invention and the idea of their purpose. Then this heap of intangibles rises like a mountain of silver, glittering, luminous, doing away with the night . . .

Who was I then, and who was my father?

And what was that city that tangled us in its muddy streets?

Heartsong

A bird sings from the tree. The birds sing
sending waves of desire—and I stand on my roof
waiting for a randomness to storm my days. I stand on my roof
filled with the longing that sings its way out of the bird.
And I am afraid that my call will break me,
that the cry blocked by my tongue will pronounce me mad.
O bird mad with longing, O balancing bar,
tight rope, monkey grunting from a roof. Fortunate bird.
I stand on my roof and wave centuries of desire.
I am the Bedouin pondering the abandoned campsite
licking the ashes of the night fire; the American walking
walking miles of dresses, blouses, and skirts
filling them with infinite lovers,
the mystic feeling the pull swirling in his chest,
a desert of purpose expanding and burning and yellowing
every shade or green. And I stand on my roof.
And I come like a stranger, like a feather
falling on an old woman's shoulder, like a hawk
that comes to feed from her hands, come like a mystery,
like sunlight rain, a blessing, a bus falling off a bridge,
come like a deserting soldier, a murderer chased by law,
like a girl prostitute escaping her pimp, come like a lost horse,
like a dog dying of thirst, come love, come ragged and melancholy
like the last day on earth, come like a sigh from a sick man,
come like a whisper, like a bump on the road, like a flood,
a dam breaking, turbines falling from the sky,
come love like the stench of a swamp, a barrage of light
filling a blind girl's eye, come like a memory
convulsing the body into sobs, like a carcass floating on a stream,
come like a vision, come love like a crushing need,
come like an afterthought. Heart song. Heart song.
The pole smashes and the live wires yellow streaks
on the lush grass. Come look and let me wonder.
Someone. So many. The sounds of footsteps, horses and cars.
Come look and let me wonder. I stand on my roof
echoing the bird's song. Do not sleep. Do not sleep
now that you have housed your longing
within the pain of words.

Ismailia Eclipse

for Ferial Ghazoul and Fouad Moughrabi

I no longer have to choose between
the Tuareg chief who never rose from bed
until an *alim* interpreted his dreams
and the villagers who stuffed their pillows
with secrets to forget what they had dreamt.
For days I have been returning to a winter
sunset south of Wichita, the sun hung
there as though glued to the freezing clouds,
its light, blaze red, filling the car.
My friend became restless, twisting
in his seat, said it was like the night
he awoke to his room on fire. I wanted
to know how and when, but he said nothing,
hands pressed against his face to shield him
from the light. By the time we reached
the Rockies, the fire was a dream he had
so often it is now part of his past.

Last Friday I was the first to rise.
I drove to buy the paper, Cairo's streets
unusually empty. I felt happy out
so early, grateful the heavy traffic
that drove me to the edge of madness
was nowhere to be seen. On a whim
I took the Isma'ilia highway to an oasis
recommended by friends. The road ran
through Tenth of Ramadan City,
appliance factories and high-tech farms.
For months I had not seen the horizon
and there it was splitting the desert
as though it were the Nile's twin.
Two hours of driving—switching between
Syrian, Egyptian, and Israeli broadcasts
then settling for the BBC, two hours
of no oasis, only military barracks,
grotesque sculptures of silver missiles

and grinning soldiers waving flags
and Kalashnikovs. The sand was luminous
as though the earth were itself another sun.

Then unexpectedly greenery burst,
eucalyptus and palm trees lining the road.
Along the Gulf of Suez, now a tourist strip,
I drove past hundreds of new villas—
Persian Gulf money, fundamentalism
and German sedans. Then came the shoddy
resorts of "Miami," "La Dolce Vita,"
and "Beau Site," crooked cinder block
cabins, humidity and stifling heat.
Rich and half-poor vacationing on tarred
beaches, swimming among slick rainbows
of ship engine fuel. It was then
that I found myself beside the Suez Canal.

As a child, I dreamt of the War of Attrition,
of martyred soldiers floating on the Bitter Lakes.
I was nine when the October war broke;
I sat by the radio keeping count of enemy
fighters shot over Sinai, mesmerized
by marching songs, absorbing words
soaked in faith and blood. My heroes
were the Algerian soldiers stationed
in Benghazi waiting to be sent to war.
One afternoon a jet fighter flew
what seemed like yards above our heads.
Windows rattled and burst;
doors shuttered and cracked,
The screeching drowned my senses
and I knew others must have felt
the horror I did. Yet later when we recalled
the war, we only talked about our uncle
who joined the Algerians' to avenge
his wife whom the Israelis killed
in a civilian plane eight months before,
and the disillusionment that followed—
the Algerians never went to the front,

but milled about the *souq,* buying toys
for their children, and for their wives
silk and satin, teflon pans and pots.
We voiced our bitterness singing
parodies of the songs that promised us dignity,
an Arab heaven on our parched earth.
And we never mentioned the plane,
that monstrous scream sent to pierce
the thin curtains of our pride.

As I was driving along the Canal
and as the awe I had harbored for this place
began to melt like a block of ice
tossed in a boiling pot, my memories
pressed for a resolution I could not create.
The road narrowed—shoulders under repair,
field hands pouring cement sacks,
buckets of sand, faithful drivers
like chased prey speeding to catch
the Friday preacher's last chants—
and I failed to see the canal's end.
Then Isma'ilia, scorched by sun, opened
with colonial houses drenched in shade.
I was told that in one of those mansions
Queen Victoria stayed when she attended
the opening ceremonies of the Canal,
and from her balcony saw the first ship—
rifles and tobacco bound for Madras—drift
to the Red Sea, in ear shot from Verdi
rehearsing Aida's premiere. But only the detail
about the ship's cargo was right,
Verdi, ill on arrival, did not rehearse.
Victoria never made it here,
the palace the Khadives built for her
occupied by a minor European queen.

I stopped at a whitewashed café
near the port, hundreds of crates
floating past. From tables beside me
I heard Swahili, French, and Japanese,

the menu offering dishes "according to
international taste." The atmosphere,
tinged with local color, belied the plans
of multinationals and tourism chiefs.
What to make of this place now?
The past masked as daydream emerging
to prove its infinity and the significance
of its mundane details like the book
of matches I still keep from that diner
near Wichita, burger and fries
with my friend. And the present offering
confusion and melancholy as souvenirs.
I watched the sun fall in the black water,
peach color sky, and recalled what my friend said
after leaving jail, eight years for a sigh
reported to the secret police. He fought
his pain by sleeping, diligently recording
his dreams, and now that he is out,
he misses that freedom, that expanse.
He gave his advice as another choice to add
to the villagers' and the Tuareg chief's knowing
how they have been of little help.
I sat longer, hands clutching the table's
edge, ignoring the almost hypnotic breeze,
refusing to surrender to the chatter
of businessmen planning the future
in many tongues, refusing to grieve.

White Nile Elegy

for Gretchen Knapp

Summer, and a woman lowers her jug to the river. She bathes and sings the word "why." Years later, I'm tired. A street stretches before me, alleys, opportunities business cards. Last week I took the flowers from the vase. Their stems dripped on the wood floor. I placed each in a different corner of the house. I said "I know you want to be together again. Convince me why." Convince me there is no river where I lived, that the woman never existed, that her name was not Zainab. Tell me why you do not believe the street, alleys, and the man who offered a bottle of wine, and a woman or a boy. The lovers you saw clasped under a thatched roof, who were they? We rode our horses all day—a parched clearing, dust too heavy to reach our feet. They were to meet us on the other side of the valley. Trees hissed. Hyenas yawned. Birds overhead, restless. We were too thirsty to cry for help. Her clothes are still under the tree. The flowers are shriveled and dry as scales. When we left I knew that I will have to make all the places I visit. That day in Athens, jet-lagged and numb, I was a ghost who saw two old men hug and hold hands. I saw a woman buy half a loaf of bread and—it's true—I waited to see who would buy the other half.

JANE MEAD

Ashley Martin

JANE MEAD's *The Lord and the General Din of the World* was published by Sarabande Books in 1996. She is the recipient of a Whiting Writers' Award and is poet-in-residence at Wake Forest University in Winston-Salem, North Carolina.

However,

what if I said I wanted
myself back whole—what then?

"What's broken, we can fix,"
the humans would say—predictably.

You have to love them for that.

Of course, nothing *really* heals.

I know what wind knows.
Tearing across the prairie,

bits of grit riding its cold storm—
grit like coal-dust, or like ashes:

What's the difference?
There's enough love here.

Incomplete Scenario
Involving What the Voice Said

The sky that is the limit is the one
sky—the moon: the same. Meanwhile
back at the literal ranch my father

is behind the barn boiling a cougar's
head. He does this for *my* love
of skulls, my love of how the curves

and arches hold. It is his birthday.
We speak by fax. I myself have been
out back picking up the frozen bodies

of birds while the thermometer
rises—perhaps sufficiently. In my
dream all the houses burn—but the people

are rescued. In reality, if the past
were a fence it would be what
they call *goat high and hog tight.*

And behind us. No turning back.
The year my father left us I
was six. I washed my clothes in The Muddy

Truckey all that summer—stripped
and sank them into the deep shore, then
tugged them out of the clay-like mud

and waved them around in the current.
Meanwhile, my mother was working on becoming
a resident of the great state of

Nevada. There are, after all, only
so many strategies available—meaning
who ever heard of the moon *as limit?*—meaning

the sky, when all is said and done,
that is the limit is the one sky, meaning
root hog, as they say on the farm, *or die.*

Point and Counter-Point in All Things

It is easy for the mind
to hold *magnolia* in its wings

at a time when the magnolia
is blossoming,—scattering its famous

petals, (famous white, rimed
with famous brown) around your doorstep—.

It is easy to understand the importance
of linen or to give of yourself

until there is no self. But when the book
is opened to the page about Magnolias

then where will you be? There is
a talisman called *mercy,* a single

blossom that is called *commence.*

Sometimes the Mind

is taken by surprise
as it speaks: *are you*

sure this is the right street?
for example—or just

cowpath—no more: a blurb,
a bleep, really, out of

the imagination, and then
once again everything is

perfectly still, save, perhaps,
a cow or two on the horizon,—

and the sound of cowbirds
in sudden excellence, where

formerly there were none.

JOE OSTERHAUS

JOE OSTERHAUS was educated at Pomona College, The University of Chicago, and Boston University. He has worked in scholarly publishing and taught at Boston University and at Washington University in St. Louis. Graywolf Press published his first collection, *The Domed Road*, in *Take Three: AGNI New Poets Series: 1* (1996). He lives in Washington, D.C., where he works for an IT services provider.

Gambier

A thought about *my* place in the long war
the intellectuals and poets fought
to a standstill in 1944;

the shooting war continuing full force,
life as we all know it half on hold;
gas, sugar, eggs, and butter scarce,

wardens pacing the alleyways at night
checking for escaping light, their cards
showing the blue silhouettes of airplanes;

who had to bear the possibility
of dying in the street, and at all costs avoid
being seen against the gray wash of the Thames.

Against this backdrop the new critics fought
for subjects not respected up till then;
one sees it in their pictures, the tense nights

spent poring over Tennyson or Donne,
mayflies buzzing at the copper lamp,
the pocked moon shining over a field

in Iowa, Ohio, Michigan.
And if indeed they won, what was the yield;
a way of living deep within the line?

When I look at one old picture, taken
in Gambier one summer night, my only thought
is God, that Nancy Tate was beautiful;

if I'd been there, I surely would have been
flirting over the potato salad,
knowing yet again that I'd confused

the beautiful with something like success,
yet unable to stop; my awkwardness
my only contribution to the night.

And there, in the dusk beneath the catalpa,
Berryman looking sly, Lowell assured,
while Tate recites the catalog of ships.

Pepper

I can't remember why I stepped outside,
but on the walk I took the camera
and, in the bluing air, with a backward stride,
aligned the moment in the aperture.

Now as I hold the picture, I recall
the heat of the evening; my flushed skin;
how, after stepping from the unlit hall,
I turned back to the voices talking within.

Beneath the sprawling arbor of the porch
my parents and the neighbors end the day
as the blue smoke from a mosquito torch
pours from its orange canister, and thins away.

They're seated at a rickety deal table
from which a late-night meal has just been cleared,
my father, leaning forward on an elbow,
arguing some point in a day-old beard.

Not to be outdone, our neighbor eyes
his swelling bloodlines as my father speaks,
and, as he finishes, laughs, and replies
that Nixon will survive the *Post*'s critiques.

My mother and her best friend listen, flushed
with the white wine, whose level, taut and clear,
rides the bottle's waist. Within a year,
her tumor having burst, her family hushed,

the friend will lie in a coma in the hospital.
Her manner in the photo thus takes on
the preordaining nature of a spell,
her gesture, grimace, thought both limned and drawn.

My parents, too, already sit apart,
quarrelling in gesture as they have for days,
while, at their feet, a child with a toy cart
toils through the steeps as they avoid my gaze.

But I can't doubt the laughter, or the ease
with which the families lounge after their meal;
the pool, reflected, chafed by a light breeze;
the dachshunds begging at my father's heel.

See how the cellar at the table's edge,
inconsequential then, lets go a drift
of black grains that swarm over the image,
with love and incoherence in the rift.

Shall We Dance

In *Shall We Dance*, the thirties musical
in which Astaire and Rogers play
a pair of lovestruck impresarios
who can't, it seems for the entire film,
admit they care for one another, time
itself is present in the scenes, shifting
the burden of their style to what they've lost
and shadowing their strange ambivalence
about the very things they claim to love—
slim-waisted, self-absorbed, possessed by a greed
for something they can't name, their only claim
on our attention their attractiveness,
they smile at one another in the end,
hemmed in by the plots of an older pair
who seem to share a passionless marriage,
and dance upon a balcony whose rail
swirls into an outpouring of arc-lit stars.
    Earlier, in a night scene, the camera cuts
to the slow-rolling New York ferry, and shows,
over the wash of the union violins,
the city, both in and flying past the frame,
as it was seen by no one at the time—
echoing; dark; the deep, unmetered roar
of the traffic breaking over the waves;
it seems for this one moment that
the real life of the boroughs might break through
delivering the strangeness of those lives,
as if we were the angels, newly sent,
who, standing on a tenement's warped stairs,
shuddered at the blur of circumstance
while tasting the boarders' palpable fear—
city of people sitting in dyed woolens
before cabinet-sized radios;
city of Marxist pamphleteers, and bosses
skimming the profits from the market stalls;
the red blush of the apples in the ricks
and blue tint of the fish laid out on ice

are now forever lost, though the low sound
of that one night, captured by accident
in a confetti musical, broadcasts
your presence like a clear tone on a dial.
   And this is how I've come to know the world,
through images in which my conscience
wanders like a beam, yet, never spent,
inhabits too the dusty screening rooms—
in *Shall We Dance*, Astaire, as Pete Peters,
dances at the end with a line of chorus girls
who each wear a Ginger Rogers mask,
the real Ginger, of course, hiding among them—
and maybe this is what I know about love,
the bemused wonderment and joy as each
dons and then takes off the pasteboard mask and curls,
until, smiling in the center ring, the real
Ginger sweeps affectedly into his arms,
with just the fraying at the edge, and the blue
spot that hovers briefly near her eyes
to show how studious their labor was
late one Thursday afternoon on the set,
when the bored crew eating lunch off to the side
became the first to notice how the trained arc lights
allowed the couple to recede, until
the windmill motions of their arms and legs
outran their passion by a mere half-beat;
but whether it was passion for each other,
fame, or something else at one remove
the film itself can't say, commemorating
as it does just the blight of vanished rooms.

ALAN MICHAEL PARKER

ALAN MICHAEL PARKER's first book, *Days Like Prose* (Alef Books), was named a "Notable Book for 1997" by the National Book Critics' Circle. His second collection, *The Vandals*, was recently published by BOA Editions, in 1999. He teaches at Davidson College in North Carolina.

Vandals, Horses

The vandals are dreaming, wolves are dreaming,
The horses are staked to their deaths.

In the poem of the vandals dreaming
A word bites through a lip,

Drawing blood. (The poem is in ruins.)
The vandals dream their arms unseen,

Dream themselves buried in the belly
Of the birthing mare, as a foal is

Torn to life. (The poem is banal
As the barn is bloody.)

And you and I, and you and I, we steal
Each other's blankets, wrap ourselves

In darkness, wind, in anything
The night will let us, to feel safe.

Do you feel safe? (Soft,
the vandals sleep.) Because a word

Is a dream of its meaning, you and I
Must dream the vandals dreaming:

Soft, the horses nicker in the barn.
(Soft, our poem begins as vandals dream.)

Abandoning All Pretense, the Vandals

Occupy the poem. They stake
Fluorescent tents around the public fountain,

Pan the water for our wishes,
Whistle in the literal night at all

The pretty boys and girls. In the morning,
After eggs and scrapple, 'round

The rugged rocks the vandals run,
Snapping towels, trampling the daffodils

The Ladies' Club had planted with their monogrammèd
Garden gloves. Then down the street

Through every town, poem after poem
In pairs the vandals rage—through the vacant

Snack bars and roller rinks, the Putt-Putts
And deserted Drive-Ins of the ordinary heart.

Where are you? they shout. Come out
And play! Don't you want to play?

(What with time left on the meter,
Clothes frying in the dryer, a chicken

Chickening in every pot ...) We see you there,
The vandals call. Come join the fun!

(What with bombs going off in letters,
What with packing up the future ...)

Abandoning all hope, the vandals
Leave the poem to us, to our devices.

And you and I? We curl into our lives
Of least resistance, giggle underneath

The blankets, play a game called
Catch the vandal if you can.

Vandals in the Garden

A riot of forsythia, a six-pack
Of bougainvillea, a giggle of pansies,

A hush of lavender. In the poem
About the vandals in the garden, the vandals

Shuffle all the words like cards:
Toad! Toad! Toad! Toad!

They shout at a cedar bench.
With-teria, they lisp

To a handful of marble stones.
The vandals scratch their heads,

Dig their steel-toed boots into the humus,
(Humus the color of dirt.)

Heart attack! the vandals yell in unison,
As though language weren't linear.

Heart attack! they castigate a worm.
(The hedges don't care, neat

As the hand of God allows.)
In the poem about the vandals

In the garden, you and I cower in a corner
Of our pre-modern bucolics,

Our little picnic dismantled by
The zigs of crazèd ants

Zagging toward their ziggurat.
The letter B! The future of my death!

(The vandals pass around the pork rinds.)
The sky's a trumpet, the wind's a sea,

O lie with me, the vandals sing.
The war is wine.

After the Poem Who Knows

What the vandals will do.
For now they have been sighted

At the mall, at the bank,
Down by the fire station,

At the high school make-out shack,
Everywhere that myth revises history.

I want I want I want I want!
The vandals have been heard to chant,

Their chant a chant heard far away.
(Ear to the ground, finger in the air.)

Above, a cloud,
A gull, another cloud,

Capriciousness. In the tree
At the edge of the stanza, the ghosts

Of two squirrels chase each other up
And up and up and up

Then downdowndown!
(The stanza ends.)

And you and I? Who knows
What we might do

Once the poem concludes, the vandals gone,
Our words remembered as . . .

Recidivist! screeches a screech owl.
And the vandals stomp onto

The scene, picking their teeth clean
With the chipped tips of dullèd knives.

And you and I, and you and I?
We ready ourselves for death

(O yes the poem has taught us to)
Pack up our little picnic, close the book,

And step into the future:
Hello? We're here. Is anybody home?

CARL PHILLIPS

Doug Macomber

CARL PHILLIPS is the author of four volumes of
poetry, including *Pastoral* (Graywolf Press, 2000).
His awards include the Morse Poetry Prize, an
Academy of American Poets Prize, and fellowships
from the Library of Congress and the Guggenheim
Foundation. Phillips teaches at Washington
University in St. Louis.

Chamber Music

Like something broken of wing,
lying there.
Other than breathing's *rise, catch*,

release,
a silence, as of some especially wounded
animal that, nevertheless, still

is conscious,
you can see
straight through the open

eye to where instinct falters because
for once it has come
divided: to cry out

could bring rescue; would
mean announcing, as well,
weakness, the very

helplessness for which
hasn't all this time every gaped mouth been
but waiting?

I dislike weakness, I
sang to him,
him taking my good arm

like a kind of oar,
and him drowning,
and the water as wide as Bible

says,
and no dove—as if not
anywhere now a brightness to

that room:
only the brawl of the wind
making its here-and-there bits of

difference—to the curtain,
to a shirt
swelling like, inside it, a living body or

a boy's hair, for a time, lifting.
World of *nothing-to-*
constrain-me. Turn it over. Now do it again.

Little Dance Outside the Ruins of Unreason

Nothing about that life
was incidental:

the night's routine of
the night leaves, by the moon, being
shadow-cast against the white sides of the small but

there

garage, say;

the heart—
that it kept beating—

Nothing was ever itself
only, or allowed to be:
if a field,

then a field

of massacre, from which the bodies
have but recently been
lifted, the trampled

grasses just
beginning their spring, back,

the drowse of the kill, after,

and the difficult-to-
admit-to disappointment
at the loss of them, carnage's
bright details,

for what they meant of
vulnerability,
that softness which has seemed the body's
greatest truth. . . .

To look at you,
looking that way—at me—

How scarified it is,
devotion's face—as from the labor of
too long accepting

substitution

over what it fears has been
nothing at all, certain

moments, of weakness.

Weakness, I think,
defined us most. We all but made of it

a country—

Let it fall.

Take my hand.

(Singing)
nothing unforgivable

(Singing)
everything to forgive

Recumbent

Here, the ribs end, they—divide, into
double fans. Splay. And fall. I believe
the pictures—there

must be, therefore, the heart
underneath and off-centered, little
down-beat,

then not. The hair: important,
but the eyes moreso, and the mouth, even
more. Every darkness. The limbs,

all along, obvious—arms, legs—
four workable unriddlings I ought not
to have had to come to by

guessing,—for so long. The brain tonight
like a cavernful of small, constant
winds in front of which the ten

answers to the question *what mattered
most and, so, defined me?* disband,
assemble, in no order, any order:

ambition;
an instinct for correct color;
sex—as I want it and, after, as I can give it;

music, by which I mean as much water as I do the notes as I do the leaves;
fraternity—of love, the one shape I've found not difficult to find always;
words, but only when ordered as—as a rule—they have not been;

less the truth, than a way to frame it;
those losses which no inadequate guilt attends;
a devotion across which, let a bit of the flaw show;

human, reasonable,
the flaws. . . .
Why regret?

Finally, nothing was
not marvelous. I remember the tongs. Clamps. Lighted coals;
other disappointments. I

remember the art of interposing
a distance between pain and
self—*where did that go?,* some part of

the brain stirs at,
the mouth holds,
the breath carries,

the cock at ease already
inside that angle I call
blunted-arrow-how-now-make-your-mark

echoes,
the backside—once
stunningly-broken phalanx, now broken

merely—also echoes. . . .
The knobs, the buttons. Iliadic,
vulnerable, the nipple. Cell

after cell, sort-of-labyrinth,
honeycomb, all the thick-with-its-own-sweetness
liquid walled in by pattern, by

regimentation until it isn't, until the walls fail,
neglected, the flesh a hive but
all the bees, classically,

smoked out.
I trusted the smoke, believed in the fire it must
mean, somewhere,

I remember the bellows—a kind of
heaven, the two hands, laboring
at them.

Regalia Figure

We were mistaken, I think.

I think the soul wants
no mate
except body, what it has

already, I think
the body is not
a cage,

no,

but the necessary foil
against which the soul
proves it was always

true, what they said: to stand
unsuffering
in the presence of another's
agony is its own
perhaps difficult but
irrefutable pleasure.

That I might not have
thought so, without
you, I understand now.

Likewise, about the body
wanting most
only another body, the flesh
from within
lit as if with an instinct for,

endlessly, more
of itself, for
a joint suffering which,

if it too is a kind of pleasure,

if also the only one the body is
likely in this lifetime to

come into, how refuse?

Possibly—probably—there
was not ever a choice
anyway.

The revised version of
effortless.

The twice-ploughed-
back-into-itself
field, the light
upon it,
the animal lives
inside the field, inside the light—

I am learning to pity
less what
lacks will entirely.

There are things worse than being
like that.—And yet,
to let go of it, ambition,
seems as impossible, as
impossible—

How extend forgiveness
insincerely? Meeting you,

I knew you utterly.
I saw, utterly,

this life.
I'd put it on.
I'd wear it like

—a crown, for
how it flashes.

D. A. POWELL

Don Silverek

D. A. POWELL was born in Georgia and educated in California, Iowa, and on the streets. Legal means of earning a living have included engraver, theatre usher, waiter, tortilla salesman, shoe salesman, caterer, and landscaper. Powell currently lives in San Francisco and collects versions of "Girl from Ipanema." In his next life, Powell wants to own a flower farm. His first book of poems, *Tea*, was published by University Press of New England/Wesleyan University Press, 1998.

[who won't praise green. each minute to caress each minute blade of spring. green slice us open]

a song of mayflies

who won't praise green.   each minute to caress each minute blade of spring.   green slice us open
spew of willow crotch: we float upward a whirling chaff. sunlight sings in us *some glad morning*

when we are called we are called ephemera.   palpitating length of a psalm.   who isn't halfway gone
fatherless and childless: not a who will know us.   dazzled afternoon won't we widow ourselves away

[what direction will you take when the universe collapses. you who when you go must go someplace]

what direction will you take when the universe collapses.   you who when you go must go someplace
you who must have more to spend than the rest of your life: busfare for instance.   mileage coupons

you have lived with yourself these several long years and wasn't that enough.   the awe now worn
behind the vacations of which you are fond: a flinch of terror.   your loins sag like a hammock

once men gobbled the garbo of you.   no wonder reclusiveness: in the russian river of your veins
the salmon are murmuring.   you go to your bungalow.   you know your bungalow dark as a birthmark

D. A. POWELL   185

[ode]

where have you gone blue middle of a decade?   the gates creak.   a sigh is so vastly different
the diary is pure spine.   in the most gingerly way each leaf opened reveals the less of you

83, 84, 85:   your relics in a converse box.   adoring letters from one upon whom you put the kibosh
shade trees bent to listen for a song.   [erasure?]   all of your best composing is lament

faithless time you steal the handsome petals for yourself.   a bruised fist of hyacinth becomes you
when the wind bears no whisper but alack: an eye fears you & distance: the short distance across

[how his body stood against a thicket. rich in hardwood gentry: ponderous and gloomy]

how his body stood against a thicket.   rich in hardwood gentry: ponderous and gloomy
the limbs would still extend a noble canopy had they not been so alluring: pitch and timber

hungry for plowland and pasture the notchers came.   char and rot the tools for clearing
driven deep into tangles the aching teams.   corduroy roads leading to the penetrable duff

he has been pioneered: given to the final stump allowing settlement.   slow collapse
these trees stripped and unable.   there was no child in him: a land traversed many times

signs dot the road where he should flourish.   could the sparse line on a sign indicate the forest

CLAUDIA RANKINE

John Lucas

CLAUDIA RANKINE is the author of *The End of the Alphabet* (Grove Press, 1998) and *Nothing in Nature is Private* (Cleveland State University Press, 1995). She teaches at Barnard College.

A short narrative of hand and face in service of PLOT, entitled,

Proximity of clock to lock

1.

In the marriage, not able to anticipate how they would feel when baby Ersatz was born, they made decisions now about how they would make decisions then.

He was biting his cuticle.

She pulled his hand away from his face.

He was biting his cuticle.

And this seemed reasonable in the midst of insurance forms: plan A with a ninety-dollar deductible, plan B without.

He was biting his cuticle.

Because the system had a doctor inside and a doctor
outside—

He was biting his cuticle.

His tongue lifted the sliver of skin liking the feel,
his tongue lifting, his teeth creating a list of tears, little rips
in the claims the birth would make, errata on his hands.
Were they the wrong hands? Botched and reddening.

He was biting his cuticle.

She pulled his hand away from his face: kept and salted
terrain: in the doldrums, characterized by calms, at a depth
capable of stasis:

He saw that where sperm dried this morning his skin
looked ashen; flaking, as if it were the dead of winter and
he did not care, as if the taste of laughter were showing
itself and he did not care.

He was biting his cuticle.
(What?) (You know what.)

Proximity of inner to in her

2.

What was it that they wanted? More flesh of their flesh?
In the days they were not careful, too much fluttering to
not respond, not reenter, not laugh and not swallow the
laugh, what was it that they wanted?

He does not call out, except with his eyes.

He passes each moment and knows it is never that, never the moment calling. It is he who calls out, awakening each moment.

Blink and the link is gone.

Blinded, she wonders away. Increasingly encased by the projected angled scar of a perhaps C-section. Surely it too will cost: a newer fear in the cut or did she cut a fear, a thought spill, involving the womb's pace, its space.

Then the anterior view:

She's turning back to look you in the eye, wry-neck bird, Ersatz. A groove in her palm says a boy will be born, says they will not be blind forever though the marriage would cry, "no", though the marriage would cry "please". And always their sighs would be the sighs that mattered.

When a breath comes would they let go in relief?

This figured equation takes Liv awry down the broad hallway (we live in each other hold each other up like able tables). She asks the bathroom to be her escape, below being. in the still. in the moment the house chokes. in the gnashing of low. oh the blue violence of true. in tolerable decision. decide a child beneath the I. unborn infant in the still illumined mind.

The moment wakened, awakening soul of, cape to warm herself. in she steps from the swarming arms of her own insides where a ticking sticks to the mind like a drip a room away. urethral resistance lowers, a stream sprays the bowl.

She lets the tissue fall, wondering, Is the new always a form of a truce? A bruising?

Proximity of stuck to tuck

3.

Liv's own mother had the smell of pee beneath her nails.
It convinced her that is how she lost him. He would cover
his lips with her hand: the nail seeping the scent of infant.
a dried, hollowing of appetite. The forgotten kiss—
resigned. dismissed. Finally and once, Liv's mother asked,

Why have you let go my hand?   Her father answered,

I, I was supposed to go and now I am late.

BARBARA RAS

Alfred Rucker

BARBARA RAS won the 1997 Walt Whitman Award for her collection *Bite Every Sorrow* (Louisiana State University Press), which also received the Kate Tufts Discovery Award. She lives in Athens, Georgia.

My Train

Just a few of us here at midday.
The Indian uniformed as a private guard is playing a radio
against the rules. From across the aisle the tinny singing
sounds like a supplicant with a head cold.
In front of me a woman with cornrows is sewing
a quilt the size of a baby elephant, maybe the flag of a ruined country,
one wracked by mobs, the kinds of thugs that give anarchy a bad name.
Her little boy is looking out over the cranes at the Oakland docks, past
armies of forklifts painted a putrid green, out toward the horizon
through the BART train window with plastic binoculars.
The white man in front of the Indian wears a white turban,
his beard reaches down to his navel in spirals like thoughts that have lived
together too long, webs that have outlasted the last tooth in the comb.
Hey friends, I want to shout, Has anyone eaten at Fat Ed's,
the stucco restaurant on the tracks
between a hurricane fence and a back yard out of Beirut?
If our car were a prison, I might be reading poems, my companions
tracing circles with their toes on the mustard carpet, and in the background
voices talking in that you-better-believe-it tone.

Does anyone on board remember having a rabbit muff or thinking
the eye of God followed you even under the table?
Has anyone here thought of jumping, tired of choosing
between lying abed and facing the day, a day that could include tiny cracks,
throwing up, or meeting with the boss for a new bout of abuse,
your mind wandering to the bodies from the wreck on Highway 49,
how their feet stuck out from under the blankets, yes
a day of choices, here the mourning doves calling at the window
on the 13th floor, there the dark beauty of the bridge at the Golden Gate,
its sweet stretch of cables above and below
the blue.
Is anyone here about to snap, heading for tomorrow's paper (section B),
or will the next to break choose the canyon of the third rail,
where the winds come before the bulk, where the onward rush
of air and metal sweeps you up in urges of expatriotism,
thoughts of a kinder country, maybe a berry boat,
your hands on the wheel, the wind in your hair,
that's where she leapt, the woman yesterday who landed
under my train and when they pulled her out
from under the first car, she said, I jumped down
to get my earring, I jumped down to get my earring.

Pregnant Poets Swim Lake Tarleton, New Hampshire

for Emily Wheeler

You dive in, head for the other side, sure
that to swim a lake means to cross it,
whole. I am slow to follow,
repelled by edgewater rife with growth, the darker
suck of the deep. You lead,
letting go so surely you possess. I surrender.
Midlake we rest, breathless, let up our feet.
Our bellies are eight-month fruits
fabulous with weightlessness.
We have entered summer like a state of pasture,
pregnancy like a state of mind so full
nothing else can be.

Sharing this is simple: the surprise of a tomato
still perfect after days in a pocket.
Here is the circle made flesh.
How much water does it take to make blood?
Where do Tibetans get the conches
they blow to release the trapped sound of the sea?
Our talk slows to the lengthening loop of the blood,
pauses for tiny hands, tiny feet, to beat their say-so.
"Marianne" lasts as long as a complete sentence
before the next utterance floats up, "Moore."
We are the gardens. We are the toads.
The season of wetness is upon us.
Leap. Leap for all the kingdoms
and all the waters,
the water that breaks,
the rain, the juice, the tide,
the dark water that draws light down to life.

The Sadness of Couples

First the chemistry that made their atoms wobble,
their money drunk, even their silverware
delirious, like the time at Café Tropical when the knife
he asks for comes all out of proportion, something between a carver
and a machete, and he takes an avocado and comfortably
cuts it into green smiles he feeds to her
one by one. Or when she took him into the wind chest
of the church organ to feel the held breath coming from the turbine
in the basement, like being in a mouth about to blow out a cake full of candles.

Next bridges, his, the erector set kind,
its machinery in a constant work, lifting and lowering,
all for the anxious ships, their sweaty metal, some days
expanding, others contracting, wanting only to get even.
And hers, a tree trunk serendipitously spanning a chasm,
papaya-robed monks sliding across in barefoot tranquillity,
until she starts across, suddenly wondering if the tree fell of its own accord

or was it dragged there, by whom, and did they get it right
at the ends, where for all she knows the earth is giving out.

Then it's galoshes, red rubber knee-highs that could have been a ball
in a different life, or the black kind that gauchos wear in the mist at dusk,
which is dark and sun all mixed up, pretty perhaps,
but what if they're gunning for someone? he wonders.
And she meanwhile is thinking about executioners
in the Dark Ages, up before dawn to chop heads, then the walk home
in the cold, the pond ice cracking like sick laughter, the winter light
a bit greenish, as if it had oozed out of the trees.

Now back in their living room, everything has become dangerous,
the dumb cane, the shine on the floor, the pillows.
She says, "I found the burnt Lincoln Logs in the closet."
He says, "Yeah, and I found the plane tickets in the freezer."
She says, "You always," he says, "You never."
One says, "Sex," the other says, "Money."
After a long silence he gets up to press the battery button
on the smoke alarm. She pours another drink.

In the yard, a child is scraping birdseed up off the pavement,
tossing it into the air, again and again,
believing over and over the shower of gold
will stay up there
this time.

The Sadness of Memory

Like bees after being out in the world, gathering and sucking up their lot,
flower to flower, it's back to the hive, a rest, then regurgitating it all,
except theirs comes up honey.
I still miss the flowers of my childhood. Lilacs. Pussy willows.
My grandfather's hedge clippings, the shiny green leaves, smaller than bay.
And my mother's wedding gown, how it pooled
on the floor at her feet in the photos and on me
anything but regal when I'd creep into the cedar closet

and pull the shimmering dress down out of the garment bag
because the weight of the cool satin over my shoulders felt like love.
Can you remember where life left off
walking daffily forward and memory turned back, suddenly aghast
at the size of the tracks, the voices beckoning behind,
Aunt Josephine's whispering, *Donuts, jelly donuts*, and my grandmother's
Barbarka, Barbarka, she calls me, Polish for Babs, and my mother's
Holy, holy, holy, though God knows why I hear it that way,
since she dropped the church even before me.
Funny how it's always the women calling, the men off behind doors,
playing cards, emptying the thermos, squinting to keep out the light,
and my father, sleeping with an arm over his face
like a wing waiting to be unfurled.
Memory, like animals in our bodies, the cat
that drops its gift vole on the stoop and there you are, back in the cellar
practicing tap dances on the linoleum in the room with the stone sinks
because the upstairs floor couldn't support
a five-year-old prancing around in black shoes with cleats,
or the dog in your mind, the one that barks you out of a dream
into remembering the girl taken from her house while her mother slept,
and you fling open the bedroom door, dash to the checkpoints—
front door, back door, windows, at last your daughter, in her bed and breathing.
You go back to your life, the lists you make to carry you forward,
while your heart's alarm resets itself for the next
ding-a-ling-a-ling of panic or the next memory, the stray,
the junkyard dog, the coyote, the wolf.

MARTHA RHODES

Peggy Eliot

MARTHA RHODES is the author of *At the Gate*
(Provincetown Arts Press, 1995) and was a Bread
Loaf Fellow in 1995. Her work has appeared in
APR, Agni, and *Ploughshares,* among other
journals. She teaches at Emerson College and at
The New School for Social Research and is the
director and founding editor of Four Way Books.
Her second collection of poems, *Perfect
Disappearance,* is forthcoming from New Issues
Press in 2000.

It being forbidden

to excuse oneself from table
before each morsel is chewed and swallowed;
it being forbidden to laugh
unless he conducts, pitch and duration,
his arms raised, our sisterly heads shamed
downward; it being forbidden
to invite another to that table who dares
to be more handsome and charming than he.

It being commanded to worship
that occupier of the armed-chair,
carver of pheasants, rabbinic imposter,
tweed-suited weekend gardener,
peddler of diamonds to the ghetto

and we do worship him
for plentiful is his table,
joyous the summer camps,
vast the Canadian forests,
the Caribbean Sea.

He who orchestrates with knife and fork
pulls us to our knees
and we pray with him who whispers
do you love me
and we cry with him who whimpers
no one loves me
and we kiss him on his temple
no one touches me
and we remain in his house
longer than we ought, for he prophesies
even you shall leave me
and when we do leave him, as we must,
we transplant lilacs and peonies from his garden
to ours so that he shall bloom
beneath our windows.

How Fast

Can you tell me where my car is,
please
and then, when I'm in it, where
to put it, which way (and how long) to turn it
from exactly where it is
and then what, what, once turned?

Can you tell me where my car is?

And my keys, how to turn *them*,
how to place my foot
on which pedal, and my hands
can you put your hands where mine should go?

Can you tell me if I am always like this,

when I am sleeping, do I know on my own
when to turn over, which way to lay my body across the bed,
which way to place my head and arms, how far
to pull the blanket up, how to rise
in the middle of the night when my body needs,
and where to walk, from bed to where? Do I call for you
even then? I'm asking you,

in this lot, near my parents' house,
how do I get to that house, theirs
the only one on the street I can't see, so clouded
it is with smoke. Which way to that fire,
please,
how to reach that fire, please, and then
how do I rotate my body, and how fast,
if I reach there, where
will I find the pit, the stake

Through Clouds, Their Whispers

A bridge, fallen. And so
they call me. *Lie across our river*, they beg
up through clouds, their whispers reach me.
Why should I bother? Why listen?
I have never been touched before, why now,
such intimacies—they explain how they'll
move on me, rolling, stamping.
They'll dump garbage, furniture, their murdered.
Some god-help-them will jump from me, *let them*, I'm told.

How do they want me?
On my back looking up their skirts,
staring at their bulging zippers,
into their baby carriages? Or turned over?
Never before touched,
how many hands positioning me?
Then the planting of trees up my spine as I span their ankle-deep river.
They will celebrate me with bandstands, dog runs, bike paths.
I have never been, nor have I, touched. Do I dare do this?

When they walk across who will first wrap her long legs around me,
roll down that hill into this river, lie on its banks, spreading wide
so the breeze of me may dry her every and all afternoon, she will
walk across the small of my back, she will lie on my back,
gently day and night I will swing her to sleep.

But if my arms tire, and my legs
and my ribs, when they begin to crack
and I can no longer reach shore-to-shore (yes
even *our* bones shrink), which of you cousins
will listen if I call upward,
will any of you come for me,
or even remember me,
how twice each day
I stand in your midst—

we scrub and groom ourselves
with so much hope, as if
at last, in these clouds,
someone's there for each of us,
for each, a kiss.

KATRINA ROBERTS

KATRINA ROBERTS was born in Red Bank, New Jersey. Her first book of poems, *How Late Desire Looks* (Gibbs-Smith, 1997), won the Peregrine Smith Prize in 1997. Currently she is assistant professor of English/Creative Writing and director of the Visiting Writers Reading Series at Whitman College in Walla Walla, Washington.

How Late Desire Looks

To begin with something not already caught
In the current of another's life, an indifferent
Hand of transparent wind playing first
With the sleeve at your damp wrist, then
Pressing strands of hair sideways against my
Mouth, the beautiful coming, like a gift
Of the rare Indigo Bunting, body turquoise
At your feeder in the slanting light, soft
Particles of air, silting through high aspens
To settle around us like hope itself. I could

Watch you carry a clear glass jar of water
Walking nowhere in particular, at least
Forever—back and forth across your yard
Where five orange poppies, like saucers
Tilt together on slender necks, and scents
Of globe basil, nicotiana and lilies intermix
Because you've cultivated this rocky, sloping

Piece of wilderness into a place to live—
Just for the way what looks in your eyes
Like thirst, holds me contained one minute

Longer than intended, since I'm a neighbor
Merely returning a borrowed bicycle or book
And even now we hear your wife's car grind
Into the drive, arriving, and the startled
Bunting, which is actually black but for a
Complex pattern of diffraction through its
Structure of feathers, suddenly takes off
So that what remains are a few Chickadees,
The most common Yellowthroat, taunting:
Which-is-it, Which-is-it, Which-is-it
And the Grosbeak with its rose-breasted blush.

Postcard From the Coast

Night long, knocking on barn boards, the scuffling mare moves
Cold molecules in a box-step her stall only just allows,
While inside her walls, sharp jabs of a twiggy leg could prove
One thing's half right in this world. I hear you think, trail

You out, tromp the tamped mud path back, frozen & moon-still.
Your breath's a snagged thread running the black wool warp of sky
& fixing my eyes on the breadth of your blades, I catch mine, filled
With the way time ratchets here, chilled slow, at least in an awed

Mind, even now . . . *If only*. Two words suspended, a clear night.
Two worlds clefting in duplicate apart. Some slight hesitation giving
Birth to cool possibility nothing would remain forever a part

Of life on tranquillity's farm. But what harm? By fall, might
We have ridden the breech foal? Might we be better near, not living
Sundered by plains as we are? *Rich dirt.* Expansive reach of the heart.

MATTHEW ROHRER

Susan McCullogh

MATTHEW ROHRER grew up in Oklahoma and attended the University of Michigan, University College Dublin, and The Iowa Writers Workshop. His book, *A Hummock in the Malookas* (W. W. Norton & Co., 1995), was selected by Mary Oliver for the 1994 National Poetry Series. He lives in Brooklyn and is poetry editor of *Fence*.

Comet

We could hitch the Horses of Instruction

Twice I heard them under the window

Under our flophouse, lousy with towels

Stamping under a moon

How many moons have circled our leaking heads and hearts?

One

The same one every night, hitched to the Horses of Instruction

It's a heavy heart they drag through the hills

My heart sinks into the couch

Yours into the sink

We believe Love lives in the heart

Which goes in and out

Why did they teach us that

We want to pin it to a constant

Let's pin it to a comet

It'll return

Starfish Waving to Me From the Sand

When I pay close attention to my senses I become immobile.
I'm stuck living each moment
instead of taking great strides across them.
And these are lonely moments.
Without her this desiccated starfish is my only friend,
starfish waving to me from the sand.
Last night an overcoat beckoned to me from the closet.
But that was the whole of our frustrating discussion.
I went back to stare at her portrait by my bed.
To fall asleep and dream of her portrait rippling
on the Ghost Ship's sails.
The rigging creaking in the dream was like her sighs.

Childhood Stories

They learned to turn off the gravity in an auditorium
and we all rose into the air,
the same room where they demonstrated
pow-wows and prestidigitation.

But not everyone believed it.
That was the most important lesson
I learned—that a truck driven by a dog
could roll down a hill at dusk
and roll right off a dock into a lake
and sink, and if no one believes you
then what is the point
of telling them wonderful things?

I walked home from the pow-wow
on an early winter night in amazement:
they let me buy the toy tomahawk!
As soon as I got home I was going
to hit my sister with it, but I didn't know this.

Precision German Craftsmanship

It was a good day and I was about to do something important
and good, but then I unscrewed the pen I was using
to see the ink. Precision German craftsmanship.
The Germans are so persnickety and precise,
they wash their driveways. Their mountains and streams
dance around each other in a clockwork, courtly imitation
of spring. They built the Panzer tank, out of rakes
hoses and garden gnomes; they built me.
And I've seated myself above an avenue on the brink
of mystery, always just on the lip, with my toes over the lip
but my bowels behind.

When I replaced the ink the sky was socked in,
only one window of blue open in the north, directly over someone.
But that person was reading about Rosicrucians in the laundromat,
he was unaware as the blue window closed above him.
The rest of us are limp and damp,
I see a button in front of us that says "spin cycle."
I'm going to push it.

MARISA DE LOS SANTOS

MARISA DE LOS SANTOS is the author of *From the Bones Out* (University of South Carolina Press, 2000), which is part of the James Dickey Contemporary Poetry Series. She teaches at the University of Delaware and lives in Philadelphia.

Milton Perry

Milagros Mourns the Queen of Scat

Cebu City, Philippines

It is the same each time. Daylight a broad blade
across the floor, then thin, then gone, the door

shutting behind her, the dimness undisturbed.
This church is cool if any place is cool

and almost empty. A few prayers, soft moths,
hover above a few bent heads. She kneels,

a series of flinches. Milagros misses
—sharply—grace, her body's old amplitude,

misses, too, a woman, an American,
she knew only as a voice, a story

in a magazine, photographs. In one,
a man beside her holds a trumpet,

and she makes singing look like laughter. From one,
her eyes gaze out, swimming, behind glasses.

The Virgin, blue vertical, occupies
a corner, hands lifted slightly and turned

up, as if to demonstrate their emptiness.
Her face is inward as an almond. The singer

also had a son, Milagros remembers,
and wonders, suddenly, about the soul

and those long intervals, bridges of pure
sound, spontaneous, leaping free from words.

Voice of cold evenings, fur-collared coats,
glittering towers, snow. Voice of dancing.

Voice a refusal of death. She heard it
and felt the atoms of her body shimmer,

along with all the struck, shimmering atoms
of the air. Voice like pomelo, mango,

jackfruit, papaya, voice like slow ripening,
gold juice, orange meat. Voice changeful as water.

Milagros knows it is her own voice, the one
she never used. When she walks home, her feet

will displace dust into the air; her dress,
a long fall of cotton, purple and yellow

batik, with a square neck, will swing below
her clavicle. She will buy warm, dense rolls

and eat one as she walks. She will shout
and shake a stick at dogs. It's time to leave.

Milagros stands. Slight exhalations rise
from the candles, each one breathing *miracle*.

Wiglaf

> Wiglaf the foot-warrior sat near the shoulder of his king, wearily sprinkling water on his face to wake him. He succeeded not at all.
>
> —Beowulf

It is the saddest part of a sad story:
a young man in an old man's heavy shirt,
his helmet, arm-rings, all the gold gone dull

and gummed with blood. The gutted dragon lies
there twitching, and cowards—seasoned fighters—
are dragging themselves, shamefaced, from the woods.

Wiglaf's own eyes saw his master's body
caught up by waves of flame, saw long teeth tear
the great one's throat. Through clots of smoke, he

found the weak spot, struck, and found out later
what is worse than dragons. Kings die slowly,
gasping words. Young Wiglaf loved his king

and carried water to him, in his hands.
This story is and isn't old. My half-brother's
sixth-month-born, three-pound daughter was alive

an hour last December, and, in spring, he's
saying this, "You haven't seen her room, yet"
although he knows I have, the crib and stack

of folded blankets, silver brush and comb
his wife lifts up to dust beneath and then
puts back. Fat bears and grinning tigers dance

across the wall. Foot-warrior Wiglaf knew
the king was dead, and still he bathed his face
to wake him, sprinkling water, while the others

watched. We are standing in my brother's yard,
where a single mimosa, bloom-decked, leans
in careful arabesque. He's choking, weary,

on his loss, and I see how love, once started,
can become a thing apart from us,
a being all its own, unstoppable,

just watching as we waste our human gestures
on the air, and who can say if it's
the monster or the hero of our lives?

Women Watching Basketball

For us, five writers, it's partly
   to do with the language, little spells
      hyphenated, elegant lingo,

words swirling like whiskey in the mouth:
   pump-fake, post-up, two-guard,
      pick-and-roll. We are casual.

Like Whitman—who'd have been a fan
   for sure, adoring and bearded,
      tossing his hat in the air

for the Knicks—we speak passwords
   primeval, we enter this world
      and belong. With adamant hands,

we argue calls, how best
   to beat the double-team, the beauty
      of an inside-outside game.

And, too, it's the players themselves
   that attract us, their lives, loose-
      linked fragments of story

each of us seeks and collects:
   the guard's murdered father, the tranquil
      center's Muslim faith,

ten-thousand winter coats
    the rookie gave to children.
        But, still, it's more than all

that. Oh, how to explain
    why you love what you love?
        Picture time-lapse photography,

the certain outward opening
    of flowers, one circle of petals
        at a time, a smooth unfisting

called to life by notes sounded
    somewhere in the clenched heart,
        the thirsty root-tips, the body

of the moist earth. Exhalation
    of a long-held breath. Green
        stem, delicate tendon,

twisting toward the sun.
    Because it's like that,
        a little, the turn-around fade-away

jumper. Though we know the ethereal
    nicknames: *Magic, Dream, Air,*
        what we want most is pure

corpus, sharp tug of tricep
    and hamstring, five fingers' grip
        on the ball—hard, perfect star—

back muscles singing, glorious
    climb through the air. We imagine
        it this way: to dunk would be life

from the bones out, would be
    to declare, *Divine is the flesh!*
        and for once to believe it, believe it.

EDGAR SILEX

EDGAR SILEX is the author of two volumes of poetry: *Through All the Displacements* (Small Press Distribution, 1997) and *Even the Dead Have Memories* (chapbook). He has received fellowships from the National Endowment for the Arts and the Maryland State Council for the Arts.

Acts of Love

you are lying on the carpet of your bedroom dead
your lips blue blue as the giraffe's tongue
the crimson noose-welt around your neck
has filled with blood your dad is punching
breathes into your chest then he's kissing you
but you feel nothing like in your dreams you think
you should be hovering on the ceiling of your room
then you remember the soul does not hover it runs
to places where it was left to play like any child
and you are running now as if you still had legs and feet
through tall yellow grasses to your favorite creek
and you are diving off the tree
from which your childhood was cut
from which you dove and lost your fear
and you felt it peel then float off
and a new you sank into the drowning immense
where you are now suspended
in the unsound silence of a nether song

holding your breath into its drowning tenderness
teasing those up above with how love fools us
with its cruelty in the meantime
your father has nearly reached his end
of hoping he could save you and he looks frightened
as that first time you finally fought him back
striking not your father but your sense of shame
that made you run away and live down by the creek
with the homeless men who fished their lives from it
who took you in to keep the creek from taking you
until in fear they cut the rope from you set you free again
and now you wonder where your soul ran to that time
then you remember it like some recurring dream
when each moment was your only memory
and laughter was your only fate
and now you rise up from the dark cold deep
gasping death that could not shake its chrysalis off
and instead of flitting off suddenly
you are staring at your father's lips
who is fighting back with tears
and who out of his worst fear is yelling and shaking you
because he has no one left to blame

Departure

you fold your clipped wings in your father's house
their rough edges still itching like ghost limbs
you lay them in a box beside a pair of widened eyes
appearing to you now more frightened than curious

in the box too the sparkle you chirped with all those Springs
from your wallet a small fistful of white chiffon
torn from a mother's dress in some forgotten photograph
finally your last pair of unmended socks

the day is baking itself into a vast mirage
as you take one last look at who you had been
there you are broken pieces and scars neatly folded
looking more like a childhood you had hardly known

you put on the shadows condemned in that box
as you tape it and bury it though you won't remember where
a sense of nothing fills you like a newfound strength
inexpressible tenuous abiding in confessions yet to be born

in your attic sanctuary your father's petrified dreams
childhood prayers caught in the grey dusty webs
while in every house mirror the wrinkled brows of new doubts
your room feels wombless indifferent a forsaken god

and beyond the verdant lawns of your father's hell
at the curb where the world once ended three wind-up crows
laugh as they peck the eyes out of some roadkill
after everything you have survived

after everything you have survived you keep repeating
believing the good life is full of beginnings like these
as you open the austere doors and just walk out
wearing a false grin and your father's face

Elegy

for Bert, Daniel and Larry

what remains of the suicide's voice is the last conversation
its tenebrous air its quiet of tarns and flowing rivers
and in its laughters the eternal peace that somehow won
slight catches of a child drowning in the soul pull you

out from silence's immensity as waters reclaim their calm
and somnambulating voices those mirrors of premonitions
where you saw their blueblack faces beneath the stilled
waters of life where you heard yourself praying don't don't

still they travel through your dreams where life and death play
blue laughs smiles of your childhood thunder of masculine rains
on their sacrifice you will be carried across this world
and in your votive strength the tremble of their lives resound

migrating dreams songs from the distant I remember them
as star-dappled sojourns a solitude earth in sonorous silence
the bonfires of their words burn on and a white feather floats
on the waters of my way-worn memories

The Gift

for Carlotta

so that I might see you
the evenings frame you in their fogs

and in your absence everywhere the requiet presence
of what I could no longer bear to take

the gifts you left understand this story
is as much theirs as it is mine

I choke this pen you gave me
but all it speaks of is old sufferings

its bitter ink won't seize my bleeding
how do all one's lies one's solitudes

one's lack of supplications engender love
that responds like the ocean's waves

it laps laments inside me
makes my whole body echo like a conch shell

even my dreams have become vast
and empty shores where I look for you

I find you in everything
that overflows

in a child's discovering eyes
in the loyalties of ancient marriages

in these reminding words that speak beyond
what my voice and words disguise

each morning is filled
with what you could no longer bear to give

I wake unestranged now to their offerings
of beginnings without ends

JASON SOMMER

Richard Hinners

JASON SOMMER is author of two collections of poetry: *Lifting the Stone* (Forest Books, London, 1991) and *Other People's Troubles* (University of Chicago Press, 1997), which won the Society of Midland Authors Poetry Award and was also a finalist for PEN: U.S.A. West's literary prize for poetry. A former Mirielees Fellow in Poetry at Stanford University, Sommer has been an Alan Collins Fellow in Poetry at Bread Loaf. He teaches at Fontbonne College in St. Louis.

Mengele Shitting

I

Taking My Name

I walked around New York half-dazed, and what
had happened? Almost nothing, except everything
looked different for the change in a few syllables.

Some hours before, twenty years old, I found out my name
was not my name and wandered, discovering
whatever happens happens in the world

and an altered vision has objects in it:
this octagonal lamppost, that car—
the wrong end of binoculars in their estrangement.

Earlier, the sharp white of a china plate
circumscribing the square of brown honeycake,
laid down by my Aunt Lilly's hand,

which I'd been looking at, seated between my cousins,
when My Uncle Harry—Herschel, Lilly calls him—
started in about my name. I'd breezed in for a meal

from an East Village sublet where I lived on the cheap
with a girl from college, apparently to let
my relatives know just what the thinking was

about the war, who was behind it
and what our demonstrations aimed to do
in addition to airing summer plans to work

driving a cab awhile and go back up to Boston
for some festivals and such. Piqued by something
I said, no doubt, and much about my manner,

my uncle, easy-going usually,
given to after-dinner jokes, laughed suddenly,
tunelessly through thin lips. "Jason Sommer's summer

plans, Jason Sommer, Sommer Sommer," he singsonged.
"You think *that* is your name—*Sommer?*"
"Herschel," Aunt Lilly hissed, as he went on:

"Maybe the man who had it didn't need it
anymore and so your father took it."
"Herschel, *du herst?*" Lilly said.

I wanted to ask him what he meant
but I was used to the etiquette
around survivors. Those who'd been through

the European fire could speak or not,
or any combination of the two. I left—
the evening anyway would not recover

from his tone, which addressed me as American
in a definition other than the one they so desired
for themselves, my uncle and my father,

in Displaced Persons camp, a new definition
Harry learned by living here and having children
for whom he really wanted a softer life than his.

In his voice I was a luxury item no one could afford,
least of all me. He intended this little jolt
I got to be the smallest cost of ignorance

relieved, so much ignorance, so used to it.
But the jolt became a shaking, widening on the subway
home with the hypnotic ticuh-ticuh, ticuh-ticuh

of the train where I remembered a queasy trip
to Canada when at the border I felt my father lie
about his birthplace, his voice odd

as he answered the guard, "Breslau, Germany."
And Harry's melody continued—from every time
I ever heard the faintest hum of what he meant

and what I was now believing, despite my efforts
at reply as I walked under the ordinary signs
enumerating, denominating from walls, store

windows, posts, and poles, seen before and read
on sight, now seen somehow unread.
Harry seemed to say: a person didn't think

and then he did—all I had to do was look around awake,
which is what he learned in hard times even before
the labor camps. As if looking around

had meant anything for Harry when he walked
in front of troops to find landmines and found
no landmines, or when he tried to kill himself

by jumping from a tree and had the branches break
his fall and the fall break his arm, landing
him in dispensary whereby he missed

a fatal deportation. I think that's the story,
which I didn't know then, nor was I so conscious of
how much our own failings trouble us in others,

and especially the young. But he seemed right—
perhaps I hadn't assembled all the evidence
in my possession. I should have known

with what I knew already, or known enough
to ask. Worse still, though, might I have
suspected and pushed away suspicion,

not wanting some ungainly Jewish name,
more easily identifiable even than my face,
ready to say *Jew* before I was ready

to say it? Though I was not in hiding,
or trying for safe haven as far as I am aware,
I also had an alias instead of another name,

more frankly Jewish-sounding,
an alias that properly pronounced
sounds German, is German.

For days after I wasn't who I thought I was
or said I was aloud, at last only curious to know
how many times I would have to see what was familiar

before it became familiar once again,
when I could stop staring at the edges of things
till they shone, outlined in a buzzing light.

Too much trouble to be dizzy with it always,
I might as well have said some peculiarity in the light
of streetlamps, store-front neon, sun or moon

combined with nerves to account for the effect, let light
be light, lamppost, lamppost. It will do if you
can get others to agree that that's the story.

Last year a river flooded through a graveyard.
The bodies, washed away from their stones, recovered
one by one, massed in an unrecoverable

anonymity. The body can shift past its name
or be shifted as mine was. If it happens
it happens to anyone, and I think now I was fortunate

to discover that my name was not mine
as an absolute possession,
to be refreshed in the knowledge

that what has been given me is given
in the grant of other people's survival,
hard won and conferring on them

the power of occasional contempt,
and if the syllables I thought meant me did not,
I can declare them to be me again—as good as any,

mine to make mine for now, can consider
myself sufficiently blessed
that the places of my exile are so close to home.

II
My Father Concentrates on His Luck

Despite nativity scenes on neighbors' lawns,
it is what we call winter break,
when we are careful and remember,
and I have come home to my parents' house
with my Christian wife and our Jewish children
expecting the usual narrative:
fragments of my father's story
told right to the point of luck.
Ringed by Uzbek soldiers pointing guns,
and they've been shooting people all along,
he's trying to explain without a language
that they understand

that he's no Hungarian, but a Jew.
How do you mime *Jew*
to those with no idea of what a Jew is?
In an old joke the most Asian-looking
would break into Yiddish,
"Jewish? Funny you don't look Jewish,"
but these are only going to shoot until—
as in some old joke
the Red Army Captain—Weinstein—
does save the day in Yiddish,
"Du bist nocha Yid?" and in Uzbek,
calling them off, so all that can follow
will follow, eventually even me.

III
Speaking of the Lost

I cannot look at Lilly as I ask
my father about his younger brother Shmuel,
whom she knew only a little,
the brother also of her husband Harry
sitting on my left. Of these
survivors of slave-labor and war,
her history may be the worst,
and she never speaks of it, not of Auschwitz
or the brothers of her own she lost there,
so it's her eyes I avoid as I break the etiquette
forbidding anyone to ask for speech
when speech is memory and memory is pain.

Alone among them, I try to think of myself
as an adult with a right to speak, a man
who has paid a price and waited long enough,
and I have children of my own, off somewhere
in the house with their mother and my mother,
but I feel like a child demanding a story,
teased with the half-promise of my father's
stories, wanting the one he cannot tell—
the one which has been told to him

by witnesses in that vague way they have
of passing on essentials only, the barest news.

I want whatever else can be recovered
to hold Shmuel at the center of a final scene,
but Harry and my father have begun
now with the boyhood of someone
who is already the hero of a tale—
handsome as he was tall, as strong as he was both,
at home in the forests around Kustanovice,
gifted with understanding the language of animals,
and I continue romance to the end,
imagining him a wild creature,
gnawing his very life away to be free
of the trap, undoing the web of barbed wire
over the window of—not a cattle car,
I knew already—a Karlsruhe freight, one hundred
tons, a number chalked up outside
on the weathered boards, forcing himself
out awkwardly, dropping—how far down?—to the water.

If they suffer memory for me,
maybe I can give them something in return,
the date they need to commemorate
the true anniversary of Shmuel's death
with *yahrzeit* candles—my bookishness of use
to them with S.S. diaries, maps of train routes.
As they grow older, more and more
they want the ritual.
I want the discipline of facts,
about that train to Auschwitz, to anchor Shmuel
in the drift of others' memory where he swims
across an unnamed river to his death
in a flood of gunfire on the farther shore.

I have a plan to follow rivers
if only on the maps, until they intersect
the lines of track, and I will have the place
he died among those crossings.
How many trestle bridges can there be,

crossing as the rivers bend?
I run to get an ordinary atlas,
which shows the possibilities in blue
meandering lines and red lettering:
The Tisza, too soon out of Munkács, or the Latorica,
Laborec, Ondava, Topl'a, Torysa,
as if I could name a river to go back along
against the current of forgetting.
Nervous, I talk and talk, babbling over
the map of Eastern Europe between us on the table:
how, rate by time equaling distance, the date
must lead to the place, but either will give the other,
how at first I thought that it was winter,
filling in with images from movies,
the shot man tumbling down the incline
of the tracks, or rolling into snow.

May Lilly says abruptly *May*
between the twentieth and the twenty-second,
two days, two nights to Auschwitz
from the station at the brickworks.
She was on the transport. She was there.
Nobody looks stunned that she has harbored this
for more than forty years. No voice but mine
determined to recover Shmuel,
to rescue the hero from her silence.
How could she have kept it all these years?
Lilly, there was shooting. The train was halted
on a trestle bridge—think, the twentieth,
the twenty-first, day or night?—
Brakes shrieking. *Polizei* shouting in German.
The splashing below in the water.
Surely she would recall which day that was?
No, says Lilly mildly, *there was shooting*
many times, many times the train would stop
without a reason. In our car, everyone,
old people and children, pressed together.
The women held rags out of the window to catch
rainwater we could drink. The train had many cars.
No one thing happened I could tell from where I was.

IV
Lilly, Reparations

Aunt Lilly, Lilly, *Liteshu*
your sisters called you sometimes

in those heavy accents.
Like all of those connected

to my father, you had several names
in the several languages

of the old region, most had
American names, too.

No one had more names than my father
since he had been on the run.

Lilly, I wanted to give you something
for my bad thoughts as a child,

my conjuring with your name
when I tried to give a name

to fear—precocious research
in Ginzberg's *Legends of the Jews*

and I had you in with Lilith,
Jewish bogey woman

from Babylonian originals
Lilit, Lilu.

She was Adam's
before the mother

of us all. Just as my father's brother,
mild Herschel, Uncle Harry,

was no match for you,
Lilith was stronger than Adam,

first wife, fierce and sexy,
who left him flat in an argument

over who got the top in copulation,
flying off to breed demons

from nocturnal emissions, screeching
in the *Lilah*, semitic night,

against whom grandmothers incanted
and posted protective charms

to save the infants
over whom she had power.

     *   *   *

I thought you might kill children,
you had such anger. *Shmutz! Shmutz!*
you screamed down the street
at your son Steven
who would pick up junk
from the gutter or
the garbage cans—

an oily piece of a sparkplug,
smacked from his hand—
Dirt! Dirt!—
the guts of a music box,
the head of a doll,
lead weights inside to tip the eyes
open and shut.

I took things from him,
anyone could.
He was available to force,
one of those people who limply
allowed so much
it was a challenge
not to bully him.

He was a version
of what I would understand
a Jew to be.
His may have been the first
life in which I was a bystander.
The two of us, small boys,
the women chattering away

around us on the sidewalk
of St. John's Place in Brooklyn.
You took him between parked cars—
the matter-of-fact, casual
power of it!—
down with his pants,
you tickled his penis and he peed.

　　*　　*　　*

Something was owed you for what
had been taken, and what had been taken?

Your mother and father, four brothers,
grandparents, uncles, aunts, cousins,

most of the family and every thing,
any love that might be unafraid,

the momentum of the everyday,
sleeping along too deeply even to dream

catastrophe. What was owed
in compensation, then?

Whatever could be restored.
Your sisters. Whatever came after

that would compensate. A husband
from a fiancé who survived,

children to be named for the dead. Who owed it?
God, the Germans, the children themselves.

Was it paid? Herschel returned,
the Germans gave some money,

children were given, and given
the names of the dead. No.

      *   *   *

I, too, have something insufficient to give,
a complicated gift likely to give offense,
or perhaps no gift at all
since I hope you'll never see these words.
Your pardon, Lilly, anyway
for bringing these things up again,
also for retelling
what you know better than anyone,
out here where others listen,
as if it were something of my own.

But what I have for you
that you will not have heard,
even if you kept up with news
disinterred about the camps,
a dark gleam of shards
embedded in the midden of the rest,
concerns the later life
of the murderous Doctor Mengele
who selected you for life
on the ramp at Auschwitz-Birkenau

within several moments
of sending to the gas
your parents and small brother.
I have the story from a dear man,
the most reliable of witnesses,
who has held Mengele's bones
in his own hands—
the bastard *is* dead, Lilly,
the best evidence indicates.
The bastard. The monster.

* * *

There may be hints that God exists in some diminished form, humorous.

At the railhead Lilly saw him first, the binary motion of the stick,
among the stumbling shoals *raus*ed from the boxcars,
doling general death and fishing for his special interests—
twins, any anomaly: the hunchback father and clubfooted son—
unrhythmic metronome sending people to the left or right
onto different lines—death,   life,   death,   death, death death,   death—
or with a jerk of the thumb, a flick of the finger in white kid gloves,
arms in a half embrace of himself, left arm across his waist propping
the right, which moved only from the wrist as he parted the living stream,
fingertip flick of the finger, jerk of the thumb, or conducting with that baton,
humming opera, *tall* Lilly thought and *handsome*, in his monocle and gloves—
not merely handsome, courtly in the way my aunt described him.

Because survivors say some of the worst of the dailiness
the S.S. enforced involved the bowels,
because in terror of the latrines at night or too weak or diarrheal anyway,
people relieved themselves in the precious containers they used for soup,
or, kept at attention for hours at roll call, soiled themselves where they stood—
or at the work details, no break provided, and begging requests refused—

bear with me, Lilly, there is a reason for the coprology, and this is it:
Years later after his brief internment, every day a new name when the
    Americans
called the roll, after his release undetected and all the years of names,
Ullman, Holman, Gregor, Gregori, Hochbicler, Gerhard, Alvez, and the rest,
he acquired the habit, a kind of grooming out of fear, of biting on his
    moustache-ends,
severing bits of hair and swallowing, but since he was not animal enough to
    cough it up,
the hair lodged in his lower bowel and grew and grew as he kept chewing
until it valved the passage closed with a hairball, *tricho-bezoar*,
an asylum condition usually of the stomach—but in this case happily otherwise.
So Mengele shitting would have to lean forward with his precise fingers in his
    rectum
to guide stools past, sometimes, of course, not stools but a pouring over his
    hands,
hot as his own insides, bathing him as he should be bathed.

Lilly, rejoice in what he felt arriving at the dispensary in Jundiai, Brazil,
the filth of the surroundings bad enough (the town itself, the outer office)—
a surgeon, too, to shudder at, small-town absurd in cowboy boots,
but worst of all when he reached the sanctum of the operating room, around
    the walls
he saw disposable rubber gloves adhering to tiles, drying for re-use. But he had
    little choice.
Here he would be cut open to get at what he thought was cancer.

So, Lilly, a kind of symmetry that will pass for justice in its absence,
irony's schadenfreude, ours by interpretation of what occurs,
as good as construing Providence out of the luck of chance survival—
yours, say, Harry's, or my father's—or constructing a God
who happens to care for some and takes care of others with a little quittance.
In Dante effluvia doesn't seem that much, serious enough for the *Inferno*—
Canto 18, Ring 8, Trench 2—frauds swim it.
Who would wish for hell just to have Mengele in it?
What Mengele did was not done to him, nothing was done to him by anyone,
but he was unhappy, abandoned, fearful, startled at the least sound:
a car backfiring, being addressed by someone unexpectedly—
a small hell in the body, such as the innocent also experience,
and that hand, which motioned thousands toward death,
those fingers reaching up his ass for years,
this thing I tell you that few people know.

JULIANA SPAHR

JULIANA SPAHR's collection *Response* was published by Sun & Moon Press. She co-edits the journal *Chain* with Jena Osman and lives in Honolulu, where she teaches at the University of Hawai'i, Manoa.

from "We"

•

The story goes like this: the light
is turned on and the light enters
the room and catches on the
prism and the prism fractures this
light all over the room. The prism
takes the light and refracts it. It
takes the light and plays it over
and over. We are bathed in the
light of the prism, all over the
room. We are bathed in the light
of waking up. This is awareness.
This light bathes we who are
concerned because we have to
make room for we who are lost
or leaving other places, we who
claim land, we who came from

somewhere else, we who are
famous and followed and thus can
live anywhere we want and we
want to live here, we who are
large with food and enjoy eating,
we who scribble in notebooks
and type words, we who cook
and clean, we who debate the
records and histories and offer
our input and retellings to make
the swirl, we who do elaborate
dances in certain rigorously
defined styles of costumes that are
many colors and textures, we who
talk late at night in bars and
consider this our cultural input,
we who together wear similar
shirts on a certain day of the
week that define us as together, as
unique, as against a they, we who
welcome the we into our bed at
night in an attempt to cut the
confusion, we who don't want to
be grouped together and so
loudly and determinedly give
speeches denying the we, we who
are I, we who want to claim an
independence and superiority of
our we, we who live in a certain
place in a certain time and are
confused about history, we who
get married and married and
married, we who rigorously learn
a certain set of behaviors in an
attempt to join something that
sets us apart from those with
whom we ride on the bus, we
who proclaim, we who proclaim
our values as culture and thus
argue that these values should not

be tarnished with we, we who say
that is the way that it is when it
might not really be that way, we
who love, we who get diseases, we
who get lost in the confusion, we
who break down and break up,
we who take drugs and drop out
and say this is good, we who are
sick and wasting away on hospital
beds with tired loved ones beside
us late at night who are wonder-
ing what we will do when the
end comes, even we who are
hugged by our parents who are
drunk and smothering us, we
who are embraced in the door-
way by a lover that we never
really loved and whose body
embarrasses us, even we who feel
the we as a part of us that makes
us too big for the space we are
allowed and that want to shrug off
this we like an oversized parka.

•

The light is we. The prism is the
space known for its romantic
associations where things grow
around and into each other. The
list of we is the prism light.

We examine the light we have
written and are confused because
we can't see the singular in it and
then we realize there is no
personal story without we.

Or if we can see a singular story
it is only for a moment as it
appears in the periphery of our
vision as a mirage while our eyes
attempt to separate the light into
its separateness and fail.

.

So we begin our personal story
with a list of who we are.

.

We want this story, our personal
story, to tell this story:

It is late at night and we lean over
and kiss, our one head one way
and our other head another way,
and stick our tongues in our
mouths and it feels strange this
way, top of tongue on top of
tongue.

ADRIENNE SU

ADRIENNE SU, author of *Middle Kingdom* (Alice James Books, 1997), has received a Pushcart Prize and fellowships from Dartmouth College, the University of Virginia, and the Fine Arts Work Center in Provincetown. Recent poems and culinary essays have appeared in *Gargoyle, Indiana Review, New Letters, Prairie Schooner,* and *Saveur.* A native of Atlanta, she now lives in Iowa City and works as a freelance writer.

Darrach Dolan

Four Sonnets About Food

1

Words can't do
what bird bones
can: stew
to the stony
essence
of one
small soul, the spent
sacrifice boiled down
to the hard white
matter that nourishes
the mighty
predator, who flourishes
on the slaughtered
animal and water.

2

Who feeds
another is like bones
to him who eats
(I say "him" only
because it is a man
in my house
who eats and a woman
who goes about
the matter of sustenance),
food being always
a matter of life and
death and each day's
dining
another small dying.

3

Scallops seared
in hot iron
with grated ginger,
rice wine,
and a little oil
of sesame, served
with boiled
jasmine rice, cures
the malaise
of long, fluorescent
weekdays
spent
in the city
for money.

4

I am afraid
I can't always be
here when you need
a warm body
or words; someday
I'll slip
into the red clay
I started with
and forget
who you are,
but
for now, here's
my offering: baked red
fish, clear soup, bread.

I Can't Become a Buddhist

because I grew up vaguely Methodist
and most of the Buddhists
I know are men who turned Buddhist

after finding the religion
in a prepubescent
girl serving prawns and chicken

in coconut milk, steamed sticky rice,
papayas, and a massage for the price
of a subway token. Because they drive

cars bearing FREE TIBET bumper stickers
but would let their neighbors wither
and starve. Because they slither

up and down the supermarket aisles
waiting for the chance to ask girls
like me *Where are you really from?* while

stocking up on mung beans and swelling
with the memory of that excellent
backrub in the hands of a thirteen-

year-old goddess who's probably dying
or dead or working for Nike at a dime
a sneaker. Because their renouncing

is pointed, because all they ever wanted
was to be different and Buddhism planted
the seed of a new Me in a stunted

self-image. Because they insist on roaming
the city in off-white robes, deflecting
the sun's hot gaze, saffron being

too conspicuous and white being too damned
unprofound and likely to be sandwiched
between red and blue in a crowd of Americans.

Wedding Gifts

Everywhere, a reason for caution:
crystal bowls, white teacups, porcelain.

Objects, which used to tumble in
on their way to the junk heap,
now possessed origins.

I had no idea what to do with a dog
that didn't come from the pound,

and now, as if suddenly old,
found frailties in places I never knew existed.
Casseroles leapt, glasses imploded—

I wept each time. I knew from poetry
that no one conquers entropy,

but I also knew from poetry
everyone has to try. Rescued, the animal
loses all anonymity

in a syllable, and the hero's nobility
dissolves into family.

Marriage is the same, with dishes and rings.
Vows or no vows, you embrace your own death,
journeying to which, you only get clumsier, and things,

which you thought mere material,
become irreplaceable.

DANIEL TOBIN

Christine Casson

DANIEL TOBIN grew up in Brooklyn, N.Y., and teaches at Carthage College and the School of the Art Institute of Chicago. His work has appeared in many journals, including *Poetry, The Paris Review, The Nation, Ploughshares, Doubletake,* and *The Tampa Review.* He was awarded a "Discovery"/*The Nation* Award and NEA Fellowship. His book of poems, *Where the World is Made* (University Press of New England/Middlebury College, 1999), won the 1998 Bakeless Prize. He is the author of a critical study, *Passage to the Center: Imagination and the Sacred in the Poetry of Seamus Heaney* (University Press of Kentucky, 1999).

Deep Shit

I can't remember the name of the gaunt monk
who stroked my face during confession
years ago in that bare abbey room,
Tell me what's wrong, son, tell me what's wrong,
his fingers soft as a grandmother's, his eyes
deep and pleading; nor can I remember
what I told him—something about the pain
of feeling alone, something grim and adolescent—
my back arched against the wall. *Deep shit,*
I said to myself, *You're in deep shit,*
though his hand didn't travel any further,
and I confessed my sins, forgave the indiscretion.
Afterwards, I walked out along a road
puddled by afternoon rain as I whispered the prayer
of the lost—something facile and earnest,

something parroted and true: *Show me the way.*
Before I knew (Who could make this up?),
I was ankle-deep in cow dung, deep shit,
my life already steeped in allegory:
Christian hunkered in the Slough of Despond,
Everyman forsaken by all but Good Deeds.
Though now it's *Midnight Cowboy* I think of,
how Joe Buck discovers he'll do anything
to keep alive—turn tricks in dank theaters,
bash an old man's face with a phone to save
Ratso his friend, who dies anyway.
I'm lonely, lonely the crazed queen howls,
root of all evil, before he presses our hero
to kneel and Joe, pure of heart, breaks free
into the sleazy New York night, his journey
to the promised land of Florida begun
in the waste he's made of his life, his deep shit:
Deep shit, or whatever it is, even mishandled,
that draws us somehow beyond ourselves—
what moved the old priest to stroke my face,
his need to touch, to be touched, more powerful
than any vow. Yes, it's lonely, lonely,
like the nameless crosses of the abbey graves
where the monks perform their final wordless prayer,
O deep shit to be sure—something broken
and unbearable, something ineluctable and long.

At the Egyptian Exhibit

> Thou shalt have power over water, breathe air,
> be surfeited with the desires of the heart. . . .
> —from an Egyptian sarcophagus

How, you said, you used to sleep—the way
the mummy's hand flared awkwardly, twisted
just so, transposings of the quick and dead
made tractable behind glass. In his day:
tombs stocked full as bombshelters, the soul

beaked and twittering over the body's haunts,
or casting off from rushes in the sun's boat.
What scares is how I see you, not cured, gaunt
as this shell, but a child curled in your bed,
your small hand in the shape of something gone
but for its remnant. As if someone wedded
these worlds as unlike as skin and stone.
Or as though the wind had stopped to trace
its image in the sphinx's disappearing face.

Floor Scrapers

(after Caillebotte)

What do you make of that odd one by the door,
his silk top hat and greatcoat folded
neatly beside his chair, a sketchbook flapped
over his knees, and his eyes: flint-gray, steady,
as if staring down his own death?

To him we are the shapes our bodies make
around themselves, the *scratch, scratch* of charcoal
ferreting its trail across the blank page.
When he is finished, will we have captured
the glisten of sweat down our shirtless backs,

the taut press of our arms at the work?
I think we will be like these ringlets, stripped
layers of pigment curling into themselves,
the window behind a frame of absence,
the floor, the whole room, awash in light.

But to be stubbornly here as this stain!
Do you see? It's not him anymore but others
crowded there, and you and I before them
whispering together like confidants:
Soon, soon this canvas will be white again.

The Hunt-Cup

It's a long time since the dawn chase over shires,
hoof-beats gathering in the half-light, human wails,
and the dogpack barking in earnest, surging
for the flash through gorse, the prey manic for its lair,

leaping over tree-roots, rifling through thickets,
desperate as the fugitive whose fear encodes the wind.
Now the escaped slave can rest on his long journey north,
the scars of chains, whippings healed to infant's skin;

now the last Jew left in the ghetto, a pack
of storm-troopers trained on his shivering body,
can stand in the open singing his lost ones home;
and the children of Kurdistan, El Mozote,

of Armenia, Capetown, Kigali, Sarajevo,
of all the cities of unremembered death,
have rewound the black scrolls of their intestines
and are dancing in the squares in a joy before language.

It's an Indian summer evening in New Hope.
And our host has served us sherry in a hunt-cup,
its sterling stem a fox's head sniffing the air
like Anubis reared in judgement over the dead

who would drink of the waters of forgetfulness:
a sweet bouquet and perfect finish. Nowhere do men
bend over their riven trophy, draining its life,
partaking of this chalice as if it housed a god;

nowhere has the wind stopped dead in its tracks,
like a mother in the aftermath of massacre
refusing the offered cup, the whole world
distilled into a thimbleful of blood.

ANN TOWNSEND

ANN TOWNSEND's first collection of poetry, *Dime Store Erotics*, was published in 1998 by Silverfish Review Press. Her poetry, fiction, and essays have appeared in such journals as *Poetry, The Kenyon Review, The Nation*, and *Southern Review*. Her awards include a Pushcart Prize, a "Discovery"/*The Nation* Award, and a grant from the Ohio Arts Council. She lives in Granville, Ohio, and is associate professor of English at Denison University.

Butane, Kerosene, Gasoline

They fed the bonfire chips, chair legs,
and dark-grained deadfall gathered
from the woods. From upper windows

a rain shower swelled, billowed down
and was beer. Beneath their feet
the earth stirred. Their treble voices

were birdcalls displaced, shore birds
landlocked, a caterwaul, upheaval
against the stars' dense glittering.

Was it earthquake, midnight dynamite
or the heavy beat of their dancing?
In the pitch, the hard yaw of flames,

in sulfurous columns of smoke,
their faces flushed, dappled by mosquitoes
landing and feeding. Their anxious

voices: birdcalls burned alive,
scattered in a puff of feathers,
as some went to gaze drunken

at the stars, some to throw up
in the woods, some toward the house,
to supervise the burning of the beds.

The Shirt Collar

Out of the least shift in the wind, out of
the hitch and sway of it through the bedroom
window, the lace collar shivers and falls

from the dressmaker's dummy
like scrap paper. Now my quick daughter,
who wants to wear it just herself,

holds up this model of the begone past,
unfolded and smoothed and petted-over.
It's like the fretted trellis that sustains

mildewed roses as they climb along
the window's ledge. But her hands in play
spell roughness, and the lace tears open,

undone strings. Together we spread the damage
on the floor, to realign the collar's wings,
tactile yarnovers and openwork,

and imagine what neck held the collar
coupled from behind, what white lawn, what gloves,
what swallowing in sunlight. Bent like this,

misbraided and flyaway curls,
she can't reshape the failing light
of the afternoon back into flowers.

They speak from the window their beauty,
their ill-health. And the dressmaker's dummy leans
in mute regard, bare-necked, skirts fluttering

around the machinery. If it had arms,
they might reach, gather her in, back
from what's unfeathering on the floor.

Night Watch in the Laboratory

The whipping fishtails beneath the microscope
were what you called me to see. A little package

of protein, you said, to describe the pure energy
unscrolling across the slide. One smear holds

a thousand beginnings spending themselves—
but see, you said, the ones who might always fail,

the double-headed, the lax, the crooked tails,
the inelastic ones, swimming in circles, their inner

compass gone wrong. They're like the goldfish
I bought once with the missing fin that swam

sideways, then not at all. But wait, you said.
Watch them all slow down. My eye pressed

to the rubber gasket, the history of a generation
passed, like the dull ache I get in airports

of distant cities: so many bodies flinging themselves
onto the escalators and motorized walkways,

so many downing a last drink before the jetway,
the precarious wings lifting skyward.

In all their faces, a public blankness lets each
hustle through a crowd. Your sperm swam

and slowed, and, as the moments ticked by
on your watch, as you held me lightly,

I saw them grow less hungry, less helpless, turn to chalk.
And I lost my breath to watch your little death

as your fingers tightened around me,
and remembered the alkaline taste

on my tongue, sour, metallic, alive,
full of the fishy taste of you.

Institutional Blue

In the welfare waiting room
           the woman cradles her jaw in her palm,
back molar aching in time

           to the piped-in music.

She's on her way to the county fair,
           free tickets and all her children
in tow, to soak in the sweat-sugared air.

           They don't know how sick

she feels, how each breath's cool sting
           bends her double in the plastic seat.
She tests the tooth with her tongue.

           Beside her, all in a row, the children

swing their legs, and finger nine-month-old
            magazines, and laugh. The clerk
lets them know with her eyes, the snap of a folder,

            that they are too loud, again.

My brother calls back this day
            as one more in the chain of embarrassments,
when my mother, to keep us calm while waiting,

            made up games and begged us: Be sweet.

The Health Department posters plastered the walls
            with civic warnings and sickly children.
We prayed for handfuls of dollars

            —at night, that helped us get to sleep—

and we lined up for the stamps
            that fed us tuna and Spam, that emaciated chicken
drying beneath the butcher's blue lamp.

            Then the door closed behind us with a click:

the hot car ride, the money, food, lights,
            sweat of the fair, a tired conjunction
of desires. And the carnies' faces, my mother's tight

            voice: We won't end up like them. That sticks.

PIMONE TRIPLETT

PIMONE TRIPLETT's first book of poems, *Ruining the Picture*, was published in 1998 by Triquarterly Books. Her poems have appeared in such journals as *Poetry* and *The Paris Review*. She completed her graduate work at the University of Iowa and the University of Houston and currently teaches at the University of Oregon.

Fractal Audition

Eve to the Archangel

I guess you were the winter, a din that hid
behind the apple tree, iced over,
shagged in cantata and crash.
Whenever I listened through the nude, the given,
branches, *you* were the single finch sounding
inside them, that song of scurry and flint.
Or maybe you were just the bird's heart,
a metronome on high, a flittering whip
in his hollow bones, privacy that flies—
all you. What I've got to say is I'm through

with through. But what I want to know is why
you still need be the sum of *scales* in my head,
this scatter of *ladders* leading up,
leading down? I keep eavesdropping
on *your* voice in *my* mind, saying *get out*,
saying *cause, cause.* Lately, I watch my sons

work all day, their sweating to wrestle
some warmth from a branch. And what were you?
Just a blade's grate, a treble bristling in *subito*,
an arch, an angel, an echo ordering my life.

Comings and Goings

Bangkok

Once, in a house I will inherit in a land I can't explain,
        I heard the shout

of meat bones offered up from the market where it all goes
                wholesale. Actually, the morning's

heat rose from the newly paved road—thin folds debuting
        into the visible—

and much later, children were called in, one by one,
        away from, because of,

the street. All day, from somewhere beyond the billboard
        of a woman amply

luring tourists to new tastes, came the sound of temple monks
        praying for their one wish—

born wanting to be born again. I'd been told their voices'
        tidal heave and dwindle

would pay the debt, in part, to whatever local god they used
        to conjure creation,

giving it their good deeds, right notes, in- and exhalings,
        short spans of the body.

Meanwhile, this week in this world, a mound of sludge and leaf rot
        caught behind the house is,

over a week's time, veiled and parceled out among
                     the red ants. And still

the black flies keep entering and exiting the air above
                the table's day-old

bowl of plums. I'd like to know how it's good, or enough, for anyone—
           this small rush into

the sickly sweet, these brief becomings, part of the increase
                  we call material . . .

Since there's also the ten-year-old girl I recognize and hardly know,
              the one who's hired to sweep and clean,

to rid us of the dirt tracked in, and bundled out, finding the floor's
           small shames. Dust clumps,

carpet threads, the bits of fallen meat scrap, all the S-shaped hair
                 that daily, secretly

escaped. What can she inherit in this country where they speak
                three languages,

one for their betters, another for family, a last for servants:
          millions of voices

pitched toward the accidents of birth? I know she could leave us
                like some of the others

who wandered down the road for a better sum in the massage parlor
             they also call a coffee shop.

Or could be dreaming already, as she sweeps, of the barker who calls
          each of the girls

by number, so that, by turns, every one is among the chosen.
               He's there, behind the strobe,

passing the bodies between one dark and the next, generation
        after generation.

And she is here for now, mid-afternoon, her small hips' swing
        a slow bargain with the heat.

As if this dust shaken from her broom could enter
        the fragile argument,

we watch the freed traces scatter in sun, then cling briefly to grass.
        We look up, then look away.

Winter Swim

Less to improve her body than to trick
its talent for pain, my mother drives her daily
miles beneath tree limbs swagged with snow,
strips herself of street clothes in the pine
and faintly pee-scented locker room, and pulls
the slick coral suit over her loosening flesh
for the work of yet another immersion.
This is what she trusts: her lungs
and how far they will take her, training
to follow the pool's scrawled underbelly
of blue lines until she can swim a full
forty seconds before turning to inhale.
And because she tries to make the smallest faiths
burgeon to a kind of science, she posits,
however unlikely, that even in this dreary
immaculate, made so by chlorine, a bit
can rinse away—if only the cramp of constant
gravity—the ache of her two surgeries.

"You see," the doctor said, "some motion,
some activity . . ." Though no one ever says
you need some relief from the common drudgeries,
from a lifetime's mild and major humiliations:

housework, failed marriages, the cyclical
stains of the body, the new dog's vomit
in your shoes. I, too, want to believe
in her bargain with the pool's surface,
the private sacs beneath her ribs
filling, emptying, filling with air.
It's only what we might wish for anyone
loved, that even their simple routines
can become ritual, bathed in some sweetness
of meaning. Her arms lift easily up
and over. She kicks under to retrieve
the forgotten prop of a child's game, a quarter's
glint from the ten-foot marker, lane three . . .

Last week, during the dishes, I listened in
when her family called from the other side
of the world to say now they were waiting
for her father to die. She could hear
the sister repeating across pacific
lines, *He might go at any time and I'm
sorry*. Slowly, we understood how his own
body's blood and lungs had surged, that night
and day, beyond the likelihood of more life.
There was nothing left but to wait
in the brief swell of his remaining.

And that's where we left it, for the time being,
the dial tone seemed to fall away from her ears
as she looked past the kitchen window's
frozen scrim. For a long time she didn't move.
I could see her face, the ice filings pinned
to the glass, and beyond that, the yard's frozen pond.

I wish I could have said something.
I wish I could have held her body to me,
fiercely then, as if we weren't made
of simple fluid and the limits of that grace,
as if she could never dim and be stilled.
Or else pushed her out to the pond's frozen
currency to watch the cold-dulled carp

we had wintering beneath an ice sheet.
In this season, they're like a fine middle
that doesn't seem to ask for more—but gets it—
each a coral or bone-blue slipper,
suspended, able to be slicked back,
with a single thaw, into the small riot of swimming.

But I said nothing and made no move
since they were beautiful,
and because of that they were useless.
Even if I had walked out to the solid edge
and called her name,
she could not have come.

Manora

One of the commonest figures in Thai folklore, half-bird,
half-human, with the ability to remove and replace her
wings at will. Traditionally, Manora was bathing with her
sisters in a sacred pool when she alone was captured by the
king's servants, and was eventually driven from court life
by an envious councillor, who attempted to kill her by fire.

At first, I had no time for their half-built temples,
        their stilted rosewood pagodas
aimed at my etceteras of air.
            I was all motion then, singing, circling
over the men beveled to their iron ploughs,
        watching the boys and women burdened
with baskets of rice, fruit, nails.
            Sometimes, picking at the earth, I could feel
a little of its gravity, still not my father,
        but theirs, rooting them to his nouns.

True, hollow at the bone, thoughtless
        of borders, I believed I owned
all space, every last bit of clouds' acreage.
            But each night I could hear their tin notes,

their music of city fires,
        the wooden drum's metronome
in the marketplace, a woman's
            cough in the dark.
Soon their sounds began to close around me,
        a sudden, almost pleasant searing of the skin.

By the time I caught the full slip
        of their dissonance—a cracked branch,
a sudden swing only they could have caused
            in the undergrowth—I sang out
to all my sisters, who flew off shrieking.
        Seconds before the frank arias of capture,
the snap of hemp and horsewhip on my neck, I saw
            each rise in her flight past juvenile palms,
water streaming from her just-recovered wings:
        six birds with the receding breasts of women.

What was there to forgive, even if anyone had asked?
        Slipknotted out of the empty,
there were days I loved the rice fields, red ants,
            the black earth thick with seed, dung, tea, rotted leaves—
a new life where nothing was deep enough.
        There were other pleasures. They sent me the boy
who wanted to touch what they said I was:
            wingspan, talon, good prey, token of air.
He had the hairless cheeks of a child.
        I made him memorize the names of my ancestors.

Soon, as if we went against another order,
        the baby came, born without its ears.
And then night visions began. I saw the king
            suckling a wild boar, a beggar
paid to scrape what was left of himself
        through the uproarious aisles
of the market, listening for a thud
            or clink of coins.
Mornings I woke to tree-swifts, shrikes,
        my sisters shouting in rounds.

I was almost glad for the final fire,
      the story and its lies beginning to burn.
Of what use is an old myth,
        a folktale's brief drops of blood?
I can hear them out to catch something else now,
      hammering steel into place,
working to gird the sky with glass. And when my boy
        died some time ago, I watched them singe
his small shape to ash. In what remains
      I keep my vigil, fly off at the snap of a branch.

REETIKA VAZIRANI

Glenn Coneau

REETIKA VAZIRANI, author of *White Elephants* (Beacon, 1996), was educated at Wellesley and the University of Virginia. She is the Banister Writer-in-Residence at Sweet Briar College and recipient of a 1999 Pushcart Prize. Poems from her two new manuscripts have appeared in *Ploughshares, Literary Review, Southern Review*, and others.

Daughter-Mother-Maya-Seeta

To replay agonies was the necessary terror
the revolving door of days
Now it's over
There's no one point thank god in the turning world
I was always moving
tired too but laughing
To be a widow is an old
freedom I have known
vidua paradisea   a bird
Singly I flew trespassing on silence
and synergy was happiness my giraffe
in the face of Africa
not the clenched teeth of a mythical exile
but me among daughters
and my son at work
me pregnant with them
taking in the glamour days
town and country mirabella elle vogue
cosmpolitan   We have made this world

brown these beautiful women
the laughing and crying till we cleared the dining table
In hotels men asked my girls to fetch them more towels
In restaurants they asked us for bread
Today I'm a civil servant on the Hill
my children are with me

From the Mall what colorful sarongs
they bring me to drape my tiny ankles
the gifts we give
to Mina a necklace of Mikimoto pearls
Tara a Paloma purse for cosmetics
Lata a pair of lime shoes for the miles
Devi gives me her eclectic lit eyes
the glamour of our wilder regions
and with Bombay weavers on the twenty-four hour looms
shocking pink is the navy of India

Listen I am listening
my mind is a journey
I took its English ships
I flew over oceans
I flew in the face of skies
orienting my loss of caste in a molting nation
my dark complexion
the folly of envy
wishing all my life to be fair
My jealous god leaves and I'm no longer lonely
Hello son this is your mother
Here daughters take this energy
these maroon saris and these maroon bras
I am proud to have borne you
When you gather around me
newness comes into the world

Dream of the Evil Servant

New Delhi, 1967

1.

We kept war in the kitchen.
She ruined dinner dishes. She broke two.
A set of ten bone china plates, now eight.
As if a perfumed guest stole her riches
so she chipped my plates
cracking her nails,
blaming anything in sight.

The next day she wanted to leave at noon.
I said, *be back by four, I'm paying you.*
She sat by the door;
she put out her hand:
her knuckles knocked against mine,
hard deliberate knuckles. I gave her cash.
Off to watch movies, off to smoke ganja.

2.

She came back late and high as if my fear asked for it.
I called her *junglee.*
Everything went off late—
dinner, the children getting into bed;
but the guests understood:
they had servants too—and yet
I dreaded her service.

She stuck diaper pins in my own children.
I cursed her openly. Who shouted?
Or I cursed her silently and went my own way.
She stole bangles my husband's mother bought,
bangles a hundred years old. But she wore frayed jewelry
hawked on the street, she was like a rock that nicked
furniture in the corners you'd think only a rat could go.

junglee (Hindi)—an unruly person, a barbarian

3.

Why didn't I dismiss her?
I don't know.
She got old as I got old.
I could see her sharp shoulder bones
tighten, her knuckled skull.
I had to look at her. It had to wound me.
Listen, said my mother. *Yes mother*, I listened, crouched in my head.

Looking over the flowered verandah she said:
Who are you to think you are beautiful?
What have you got to show?
Go sit on your rag.
All my life I tended to looks,
they betrayed me. I bore you.
I am wretched. Be my mother. Be my maid.

Maya to Herself and Then to Her Gardener

Grass cut trees need pruning
I was unsure of myself Hence this garden
World I did wallow
envied my daughters My son loyal no
matter what relations my spurned self ruined
I offered empty hands and he brought me his son I have sinned

Such ingratitude I had wanted to resist it
wanted to carry my own weight
When my bones give for lack of milk
I'll still binge on coffee to wake me up cocktails to put me down
It is Saturday Mike come in
For years we puttered over azaleas out front pachysandra out back

Have I paid you sufficiently? will you come back next week or after depending
    on the rain?
Why do you never pocket my tip?
Ah you were always like me guided by the paranoia that lurks near love
No it's not too early I have
already made a pot of coffee have some I am up

E-Mail

Lastly, Marvelous, I wanted to be rich.
I would give you money to burn
and fly you to me.

That's a lie!
It was only a partly charitable wish.
I wanted to eat and dress like a pharoah or rani,
to be part of that drama in the elevator at Tiffany's.

Do I covet money?
Of course! To fly over.
Wouldn't it be nice to get in bed,
listen to Ella and Louis, and neck all night?

What a wonderful century:
think of all its glory and how we forgot
the color of our skins, religions, regrets,
our million defects, blew out of a volume of history.

KAREN VOLKMAN

Richard Meier

KAREN VOLKMAN was born in Miami in 1967 and was educated at New College, Syracuse University, and the University of Houston. Her first book of poems, *Crash's Law* (W. W. Norton), was a 1995 National Poetry Series selection. Her poems have appeared in many literary publications, including *Poetry, Paris Review*, and *American Poetry Review*. She received an NEA Fellowship and has been a resident at the MacDowell Colony and Yaddo.

Create Desire

Someone was searching for a Form of Fire.
Bird-eyed, the wind watched.
Four deer in a blowsy meadow.
As though it were simply random, a stately stare.

What's six and six and two and ten?
Time that my eye ached, my heart shook, why?
Mistaking lime for lemon.
Dressed in cobalt, charcoal, thistle—and control.

If they had more they would need less.
A proposal from the squinting logician.
Seems we are legal, seems we are ill.
Ponderous purpose, are you weather, are you wheel?

Gold with a heart of cinder.
Little blue chip dancing in the light of the loom.
Mistress, May-girl, whom will you kiss?
The death of water is the birth of air.

Untitled

Shrewd star, who crudes our naming: you should be flame. Should be
everyone's makeshift measure, rife with tending—constellations called *Scatter*
or *Spent Memory* or *Crown of Yes* or *Three Maids Slow in Pleasure.* Some days
my eyes are green like verdigris, or green like verdant ardor, or like impair.
Does it matter the law is a frame to hang your heart in? This *was.* I saw it,
schemed it, bled it. I was *then.* Or: I ran with all my leagues of forgotten steps
to reach you. A rose said to a rumor, is fame what blooms with flanged petals,
or is that cause? Are blind bones brighter in skulled winter or spring-a-dazing?
I am asking the most edgeless questions, so words will keep them, so the green
gods in my mind will lull and lie. But constellation *Mute Cyclops*, my ravaged
child, weeps every eye.

Untitled

There comes a time to rusticate the numbers. The way the birds, jug
jug, mount in steepleless processions, or the barely comprehensible division of
our hands. Or the cliff with the face of a galled god, appalling. And these are
boundable, we count them, each and each.

But my zero, windy and sleepless, how to teach it? It speaks to the
rain, the spare precipitation—it says, Desert conditions, but I fathom the
sea—and rain in its meticulous sermon mumbles back. Talk, talk, in shrill
slaps, in strident speculations. As the almond trees flash the gold, precocious
blossoms our cold maids call blind psyche. And this was me. I give you my
digital, my radial, my baldest baby. While annul! cries the fitful keeper, who
sears and scalds. But my zero, sum and province, whole howl, skies the all.

Untitled

If it be event, I go towards and not back. I go tower, not floor.
I listen but rarely learn, I take into account occasionally, but more often there
are lips to kiss, words to pass from tongue to mouth, white entire. It knows a
few names about what I am, it goes door to door saying *She is* or *Her ire*. But
when the rainbows are handles I hold dragging earth to more vivid disasters,
oh swinging by the strap. You thought she was a dimwit flapper, really she's a
chemist with a taste for distress. You thought she came with guarantees, really
she's your nightmare hatcheck has a vagrant head. I sort of sometimes go by
the book, the need to move being visage, mask you wear like dark sky or
water (water that boils or breaks or scares the flame). We don't need a nest to
grow in, a bed to sleep. In the clairvoyance of loving wrongly, o glass pillow
o swallow, is dream is dare is dagger. Your turn.

ANTHONY WALTON

Elizabeth Leonard

ANTHONY WALTON is the author of *Mississippi: An American Journey* (Random House, 1996), co-editor, with Michael Harper, of *The Vintage Anthology of African Poetry 1750–2000* (Vintage, 1999) and *Every Shut Eye Ain't Asleep: An Anthology of Poetry by African Americans Since 1945* (Little Brown, 1994). He is the recipient of a 1998 Whiting Writer's Award and teaches at Bowdoin College.

Dissidence

in memoriam Thelonious Monk

You have to be able to hear past the pain, the obvious
minor-thirds and major-sevenths, the merely beautiful

ninths; you have to grow deaf to what you imagine
are the sounds of loneliness; you have to learn indifference

to static, and welcome noise like rain, acclimate
to another kind of silence; you have to be able to sleep

in the city, taxis and trucks careening through your dreams
and back again, hearing the whines and sirens and shrieks

as music; you must be a mathematician, a magician
of algebra, overtone and acoustics, mapping the splintered

intervals of time, tempo, harmony, stalking or sluicing blues
scales; you have to be unafraid of redundance, and aware

that dissonance-driven explorations of dissonance
may circle back to the crowded room of resolution;

you have to disagree with everything except the piano, black
and white keys marking the path you must climb step

by half-step with no compass but the blues, no company
but your distrust of the journey, of all that you hear, of arrival.

Third Shift

Mickey says hey
you guys, go throw
eleven, which means
for me and Knox to unstack
and stack a hundred
hundred pound sacks
of corn starch or dextrose,
or whatever,
off a truck out of St. Louis
or Decatur or Kansas City.
Midnight, and we will be
loading and unloading
until dawn.
Next it might be barrels
of animal fat bound
for Memphis, or sifted grain
destined to become cereal
for the breakfasts
of the middle west.
We don't know
or care, we just throw it,
get out of the way,
and stand on the dock
taking deep breaths and waving
the next guy in.
Then maybe it's break,

Knox and me on the roof,
him smoking and singing
about some woman or another
and making bad jokes about misery
loving company. I smile,
and because he knows
it will make me laugh,
he sings "Since I Fell For You"
off-key and with the wrong
words, and I look out over
the highway toward Iowa,
wondering which headlights
are headed here. Then I take
a hit, and it's time to go back.
It is always time to go back,
I am thinking of a night
when I was younger and didn't know
that life could be like this,
how I took Amtrak out of South
Bend, coming home to bury
my best friend. In Chicago
the train stopped behind a mill
on 35th Street
and I could see a man sweating
and stoking a blast furnace.
It was August, the sky going
orange to pink, and it looked
like he was working the gates
of hell. I am learning to think
of these gates as such, because
it's hotter than hell,
Mickey is cursing the day
he was born, Knox is singing
about misery, which is its own
company, and two more trucks
are backing in, steady
as the gravity dragging us
into the ground.

JOE WENDEROTH

JOE WENDEROTH grew up near Baltimore, Maryland. His first book of poems, *Disfortune*, was published by Wesleyan University Press in 1995. His other books include *It Is If I Speak* (University Press of New England/Wesleyan University Press, 2000) and a chapbook, *The Endearment* (Shortline Editions, 1999). Wenderoth lives in Mt. Horeb, Wisconsin, and Marshall, Minnesota, where he is assistant professor of English at Southwest State University.

Billy's Famous Lounge

I respect the dumb bastards.
Their faces floating in want
give me the strength
of the real current.
The current which would enter itself
as though it was not itself,
enter it from behind,
from under, standing up,
with a hand, face, tongue,
or the unspeakable soft root of names. . . .

We float this way, in want,
in the length of the loud pause.
Each chord of the electric guitar is a white petal
placed on real time, a moment,
already sinking.
The dumb bastards like the way
night's surface holds the petals up

and moves them—shows them up against the fact
of their endless disappearance.
They understand very well
it's all founded on a drain—
it carries us back and further down *in*
to where we just were,
where we're too bright to speak,
too dark to be spoken.
Where one wants only to go down,
and where one does go down.

I respect no one
more than the dumb bastards.

First Impression

I don't like my teeth. I feel they are too small. They give the wrong impression.
They mislead. And my nose—it conveys nothing of what I truly am. Come to
think of it, my face, taken as a whole, is rather unattractive, and gives the on-
looker a very wrong impression of my essence. I won't even go into my torso, or
what there is beneath. It's as if someone had quite consciously designed these
things in order to conceal me—as if, prior to my every appearance in the world,
someone was able to get inside me and fit me with a subtle disguise. I have
never fully understood these disguises, let alone been able to remove them.
Each night I dream of shaving my head, removing my teeth, my eyes, my
tongue, folding my legs up under me, placing my hands behind my back, and
covering my skin with ashes. It isn't so much that I want you to see me as hor-
rific—as the final figure in a dream of this kind. No, I want you to see me as no
different from yourself—I want you to see that I am, like you, mostly just the
dream itself, that slow brutal vanity wherein the deft dissembling of disguises is
as constant as it is unprecedented.

As Hour and Year Collapsed

We were a whole army underground;
we did not move.
We were replicas, at first,
but the army above,
that which we were shaped to resemble,
moved, spoke, faded, and came
to rot
in shallow graves above us.
We were never them;
even as the workers painted our eyes
the colors of their eyes,
even as they hauled us by torch-light
into the vast royal burial chambers
and made us to stand the way they stood,
once, above,
we were never them.
When our faces were finally finished
and our ranks were formed,
we stood guard over the absence
of the one who required us.
No one was allowed to look.
The chambers were sealed
and the last few torches burned down.
We stood suddenly alone in silent darkness.
We knew, though, that someone above
could imagine us, and we could sleep
standing up
in that image.
The workers, who painted our eyes
and carved our horses' manes,
could imagine us—the priests,
who looked into our faces and blessed us
before and for this dark, could imagine,
and knew that we were there.
But then they moved, faded, and came to rot.
We were still spoken of, as time passed,
but only as an *idea*, as though

we did not actually stand here
inside the earth, in these colors,
these unseeing eyes, this dark.
No one any longer imagined us as real;
we had to imagine ourselves—
the way we looked, the way we stood—
from the inside,
from the stillness of our own hearts.
And we did learn to see ourselves in this way:
blind, colorful, standing guard over nothing.
And we came to accept,
as *hour* and *year* collapsed
into one dull drizzle of dust,
that we would not be found—
our guard would never be relieved.
There are worse fates than this,
we told ourselves, and we believed it, too,
until the sharp light that forged us
fell hard on our faces again
and reminded us that what we have understood
has never been what we are.

Moon River

what is true
is what seems
in a given moment
to repeat itself
without mercy
—the house
—the way the snow
has not shifted
—the few songs
that mimic the few seasons
we can bear to call
by name

My Life

after Henri Michaux

Somehow it got into my room.
I found it, and it was, naturally, trapped.
It was nothing more than a frightened animal.
Since then I raised it up.
I kept it for myself, kept it in my room,
kept it for its own good.
I named the animal, My Life.
I found food for it and fed it with my bare hands.
I let it into my bed, let it breathe in my sleep.
And the animal, in my love, my constant care,
grew up to be strong, and capable of many clever tricks.
One day, quite recently,
I was running my hand over the animal's side
and I came to understand
that it could very easily kill me.
I realized, further, that it *would* kill me.
This is why it exists, why I raised it.
Since then I have not known what to do.
I stopped feeding it,
only to find that its growth
has nothing to do with food.
I stopped cleaning it
and found that it cleans itself.
I stopped singing it to sleep
and found that it falls asleep faster without my song.
I don't know what to do.
I no longer make My Life do tricks.
I leave the animal alone
and, for now, it leaves me alone, too.
I have nothing to say, nothing to do.
Between My life and me,
a silence is coming.
Together, we will not get through this.

GREG WILLIAMSON

GREG WILLIAMSON, born in 1964, grew up in Nashville, Tenn. He teaches in the Writing Seminars at the Johns Hopkins University.

Bodies of Water

> Glimmerings are what the soul's composed of.
> —Seamus Heaney

Yes, but the body is made of water. That's
      A fact. It freezes with fear
And boils with rage because it has its states.
      It blows off steam. It swells with pride.
          It sweats like a pipe,
          But it is water.

Genetic pool, swamp of desires, its heart
      Melts at a beautiful face;
Turned to a puddle, it stands in the street and admires.
      The body runs hot and cold and down
          In soaked beds,
          Seeking its level.

There have been souls who drowned in pity, drowned
          In sorrow. Just last week,
There was a glimmer of something out on the surface,
      Then it went under. When divers went in
              They found gold teeth
              And hundreds of miles of water.

On His Birthday

Having enjoyed his shower, the cake of soap,
The buttery toast to which he raised his cup
Of tea, having discarded the envelope
Of sugar and perused the horoscope,
          "Big deal at work turns up,"

And having lit the citronella candle
And wandered to the garden plot to check
The ripening tomato vines that dandle
Emerald solitaires, he loosens a sandal
          And sits to enjoy the deck.

If the sun's a gift, rising above the gable,
If begonias in the window bloom like bows,
If liriope turns to ribbon, it's a fable
And he's the intrusive speaker. At the table
          He sets the cards in rows,

And instantly the catalpa's full of hearts,
Exclusive clubs of finch and chickadee
Shuffle around the feeder, playing their parts
In the running commentary, which imparts:
          Black two on red three.

The grass is wet with diamonds, and the spade
In the ground he calls a spade. The serpentine
Hose is a six on which a pothook's played
By the one-eyed jack, who never learned a trade.
          Red eight on black nine.

Big deal at work. If things turned up they'd find
The clouds of icing turn to floating cakes
Of French vanilla, layered and refined.
What turns up next, what comes to the floating mind,
       Is he and the clouds are fakes.

They might be sawdust clouds of cabinetwork,
Cities of smog, exhaust, the thick cascade
Of refinery smoke, lobbies where bankers smirk.
Black seven on red eight. Big deal at work.
       He never learned a trade.

And soon enough the sun will set. The vines
Will drop their fruit. The bows will fall. The fall
Will see the birds depart, as he cosigns
Another loan, in a distant place. The signs
       Are there. If you can call

It work, he sees how the pattering mind will cope
With what the heart is feeling, like reading a cup
Of tea leaves, cloud banks, cards, the horoscope.
He shuffles the deck. He'll play his cards and hope
       Whatever he needs turns up.

Kites at the Washington Monument

> What's up, today, with our lovers?
> —W. D. Snodgrass

At fingertip control
    These state-of-the-art stunt kites
Chandelle, wingover, and roll
    To dive from conspicuous heights,

Whatever the pilots will,
    While the wowed audience follows
As the kites come in for the kill
    And slice up the air like swallows.

But, look, across the park
        Someone has put together—
What is it?—it looks like a lark
        Tossed up into the weather.

It's homemade out of paper
        That tumbles and bobs like a moth
On another meaningless caper.
        Why, it's a bit of froth

Spun on a blue lake,
        A name or a wrinkled note
Dropped into the wake
        Of an ocean-going boat.

But still it pulls itself higher
        As he would pull it back.
The line goes tight as wire,
        Or sags, falling, and goes slack,

And while the audience claps
        At the aerobatic buzz,
It flutters, quiets, then it snaps.
        But that's about all it does.

Flying its tail of rags
        Above these broken lands,
It's one of those white flags
        For things that are out of our hands,

The hoisted colors of
        Attenuated hope,
The handkerchief of a love
        That's come to the end of its rope.

When the line breaks, the string
        Floats to the ground in the wind.
He stands there watching the thing
        Still holding up his end

As the kite heads into the sky
        Like a sail leaving a slip.
The rags wave goodbye.
        They're scarves at the back of a ship.

Origami

The kids are good at this. Their nimble fingers
Double and fold and double fold the pages,
Making mimetic icons for all ages.
The floor of the school is littered with dead ringers:

Songbirds that really flap their wings, rare cranes,
Bleached bonsai trees, pale ghouls, two kinds of hats,
Dwarf stars, white roses, Persian copycats,
Small packet boats, whole fleets of flyable planes.

Some of the girls, some of the older ones,
Make effigies of boys and . . . "Goodness sakes!"
They ask what I can make. "I make mistakes."
"No, really, Mr. Greg!" They don't like puns.

I tear out a page and say, "I've made a bed."
They frown at me. I'll have to lie on it.
"See, it's a sheet." But they're not buying it,
And seem to imply ("You crazy!") it's all in my head.

I head for home, where even more white lies
Take shape. The page is a window filled with frost,
An unformed thought, a thought I had, but lost.
The page is the sclera of someone rolling his eyes

As it becomes (you'll recognize the trick)
Tomorrow morning, laundry on the line,
The South Pole, circa 1929,
The mainsail of the *Pequod*, Moby Dick,

The desert sand, the shore, the arctic waste
Of untold tales, where hero and author together
Must turn, out of the silence, into the whether-
Or-not-they-find-the-grail. Not to your taste?

The page is a flag of surrender. I surrender—
To the rustle of programs before a serious talk,
The sound of seashells, seas, the taste of chalk,
The ghost of snow, the ghost of the sky in December,

And frozen surfaces of ponds, which hide
Some frigid stirring, something. (What have I done?)
It's the napkin at a table set for one,
The shade drawn in a room where someone died.

The pages keep on turning. They assume
More shapes than I can put my fingers on,
A wall of silence, curtains, doors, false dawn,
The stared-at ceiling of my rented room.

"You crazy, Mr. Greg." The voices call;
The sheet on the unmade bed is gone awry.
I sit at my little desk in mid-July,
Throwing snowballs at the Sheetrock wall.

MARK WUNDERLICH

Tracy K. Smith

MARK WUNDERLICH is the author of *The Anchorage*, published in 1999 by the University of Massachusetts Press. Born in Fountain City, Wisconsin, he was educated at the University of Wisconsin and Columbia University. He has been a fellow at the Fine Arts Work Center in Provincetown and the recipient of the Writers at Work Poetry Fellowship and a Wallace Stegner Fellowship from Stanford University. He has published individual poems in *The Paris Review, Boston Review, Yale Review*, and *Poetry* and in various anthologies. He lives in San Fransciso.

Chapel of the Miraculous Medal

C. calls to tell me Mercury is in retrograde, so watch out. Just last night, walking up the subway stairs at 14th Street, some guy reaches under her skirt and grabs her. *You see? The whole city is nuts. Who was that guy? What a freak!* she says.

And that old apartment in Chicago, three rickety stories up, the man across the street baring himself to me every morning at 7, and again evenings at 6:30, waiting for my light to go on; his glassed-in want a naked torso behind the window. I never saw his face, just the activity, not even distance or geography could prevent him from gesturing.

In Paris there is a convent on the rue du Bac where the body of a saint lies under glass, resisting decay for a century. The nun stubbornly holds on to form, waxy hands clasped over her heart, an insect in amber.

I can barely write this to you. There was a boy. At a bar, he spoke to me, so young, mistaking me for someone younger, and groping him in the corner, his soft mouth on mine, I swear I'd forgotten how it could be, so necessary. I left him there, whispered in his ear, and hurried back to my empty rooms.

I was walking along the piers, all the men on rollerblades, the orange sun dipping down orange-red into New Jersey, and I was back in the attic room I rented from—Rose, that was her name, calling upstairs to ask if I'd like a tomato. She must have had an extra from the garden, and when I opened the door an hour or so later, it was nested in my shoe. Red, as big as my fist, one perfect thing left there just for me.

Difficult Body

A story: There was a cow in the road, struck by a semi—
half-moon of carcass and jutting legs, eyes
already milky with dust and snow, rolled upward

as if tired of this world tilted on its side.
We drove through the pink light of the police cruiser
her broken flank blowing steam in the air.

Minutes later, a deer sprang onto the road
and we hit her, crushed her pelvis—the drama reversed,
first consequence, then action—but the doe,

not dead, pulled herself with front legs
into the ditch. My father went to her, stunned her
with a tire iron before cutting her throat, and today I think

of the body of St. Francis in the Arizona desert,
carved from wood and laid in his casket,
lovingly dressed in red and white satin

covered in petitions—medals, locks of hair,
photos of infants, his head lifted and stroked,
the grain of his brow kissed by the penitent.

O wooden saint, dry body. I will not be like you,
carapace. A chalky shell scooped of its life.
I will leave less than this behind me.

On Opening

Look at it, the season's shifting.
I can see it from this slice of window—
fires smoldering on the hillside
and smoke rising up in feeble questions.

A dark house in the distance ignites
its one tinny light
and I think of light and the way
it can come too close like an enemy

or ice. Outside the wind sings
the way a door sings on opening
and all day the hammer tap
in the next room is a heartbeat

sealing in the blood then giving in,
hungry for zero. I must tell you how willingly
the body will empty itself of itself.
Cancer coils in a distant cell,

blue veins snake to a quieter place
while the night's single white sheet
stretches out wrinkle-less, chilled,
the snow fields hoarding

their empty white bowls.
Listen to that whispering!
It is the lungs casting in and out—
a spidery black spot clings to pink.

Simplify Your Combination Therapy

Two men embrace on the billboard, their faces
clean, turned hopefully toward the new millennium
and in their two public dimensions, they indicate
what luck and pharmacology might do for anyone

that handsome. Something has been tricked.
Some storm twisted its mass out over open water.
The men hold their papery faces to the bleaching sun
its damage suddenly of no consequence to the one

or two men we recognize as come back,
those who have dropped in on their lives again,
pack of donuts in a bag to help their medicine
go down. The fury has died away. What once

lit our dark apartments like a devil
has been bathed in chemicals, calmed
in ten day cycles to lighten the viral load.
Anything can be suppressed in this new world.

Take these two pills, reduced from a previous three
and place them on the tongue. Wash them back
with filtered water. Eat some fat. Together
they are your future, short-lived and American.

Acknowledgments, continued from page iv

Julie Fay, "Flowers," "Stereograph: 1903," "Santorini Daughter," and "The Mother of Andromeda" are from THE WOMAN BEHIND YOU, by Julie Fay, © 1998. Reprinted by permission of the University of Pittsburgh Press.

Chris Forhan, "The Taste of Wild Cherry," "Without Presumptions," and "Big Jigsaw," from *Forgive Us Our Happiness*, 1999, University Press of New England.

James Harms, "Sky," "Reel Around the Shadow," "As Always," and "The Joy Addict," reprinted from Jim Harms: *The Joy Addict* by permission of Carnegie Mellon University Press © 1998 by Jim Harms.

James Kimbrell, "Mt. Pisgah," "Self-Portrait, Jackson," and "A Slow Night on Texas Street," are reprinted from *The Gatehouse Heaven*, by James Kimbrell, published by Sarabande Books, Inc. © 1998 by James Kimbrell. Reprinted by permission of Sarabande Books and the author.

m loncar, "as my cat eats the head of a field mouse he has caught," "peoria," "kentucky," and "one night america: a boy and his blowtorch," from *66 galaxie*, 1998, University Press of New England/Middlebury College Press. © m. loncar.

James Longenbach, "What You Find in the Woods," from *Threshold*, 1998, University of Chicago Press.

Khaled Mattawa, "Ismailia Eclipse" and "White Nile Elegy," from *Ismailia Eclipse*, 1995, Sheep Meadow Press.

Joe Osterhaus, "Gambier," and "Pepper," from *The Domed Road*, in TAKE THREE, Agni New Poets Series: 1, 1996, Graywolf Press. Used with permission.

Alan Michael Parker, "Vandals, Horses," "Abandoning All Pretense, the Vandals," "Vandals in the Garden," After the Poem Who Knows," copyright © 1999 by Alan Michael Parker. Reprinted from THE VANDALS with the permission of BOA Editions, Ltd.

D. Powell, "[who won't praise green ...]," "[what direction will you take ...]," "[ode]," and "[how this body stood against ...]," from *Tea*, 1998, University Press of New England/Wesleyan University Press. © D. A. Powell.

Barbara Ras, "My Train," "Pregnant Poets Swim Lake Tarleton, New Hampshire," "The Sadness of Couples," and "The Sadness of Memory," from *Bite Every Sorrow*, 1998, Louisiana State University Press. Used with permission.

Katrina Roberts, "How Late Desire Looks," is taken from the award-winning poetry volume *How Late Desire Looks* by Katrina Roberts (Salt Lake City: Gibbs Smith, Publisher, 1997). Used with permission.

Marissa de los Santos, "Wiglaf," "Women Watching Basketball," and "Milagros Mourns the Queen of Scat," from *From the Bones Out*, 1999, University of South Carolina Press.

Jason Sommer, "Mengele Shitting," from *Other People's Trouble*, 1997, University of Chicago Press.

Adrienne Su, "Four Sonnets About Food" from *Middle Kingdom*, 1997, Alice James Books, University of Maine at Farmington. Reprinted with permission by Alice James books.

Daniel Tobin, "Deep Shit," "At the Egyptian Exhibit," and "The Hunt-Cup" from *Where the World Was Made*, University Press of New England. Forthcoming.

Ann Townsend, "Night Watch in the Laboratory" and "Instutional Blue" from *Dime Store Erotics*, 1998, Silverfish Review Press. Reprinted with permission.

Pimone Triplett, "Fractal Audition," "Comings and Goings," "Winter Swim," and "Manora," from *Ruining the Picture*, 1998, TriQuarterly Books, Northwestern University Press, © 1998 by Pimone Triplett.

Joe Wenderoth, "Billy's Famous Lounge," "First Impression," "As Hour and Year Collapsed," and "My Life," from *It Is If I Speak*, 2000, University Press of New England/Wesleyan University Press.

Mark Wunderlich, "Chapel of the Miraculous Medal," "Difficult Body," and "On Opening" are reprinted from Mark Wunderlich's *The Anchorage*. (Amherst: University of Massachusetts Press, 1999. Copyright © 1999 by the University of Massachusetts Press.)

Poems previously have appeared in the following publications:

Agni
American Poetry Review
The Boston Book Review
Chicago Review
College English
Columbia
Crab Orchard Review
Fence
The Formalist
Gargoyle
Harvard Review
Hootenanny
Indiana Review
The Iowa Review
JAMA: The Journal of the American Medical Association
The Journal
The Kenyon Review
The Literary Review
Many Mountains Moving
Marlboro Review
Massachusetts Review
Membrane
The Missouri Review
The Nation
New England Review
New Letters
The New Republic

New Virginia Review
The New Yorker
The Painted Bride Quarterly
The Paris Review
Parnassus
Phoebe
Pirogi Press
Pivot
Ploughshares
Poetry
Prairie Schooner
Quarterly West
Raritan Review
River Styx
Salamander
Salmagundi
Seneca Review
Slate
The Sonora Review
Southwest Review
Sycamore Review
Tamaqua
Tar River Quarterly
TriQuarterly
Verse
Western Humanities Review
Witness